GREAT

A Guide to Acquiring Shooting Skills for Big-Game Hunters

Paul C. Carter

©Copyright 2009 by Paul C. Carter

ISBN 1-4392-4701-3

All rights reserved. No part of this book may be reproduced by any mechanical, photographic, or electronic process, or in the form of a phonographic recording, nor may be it stored in a retrieval system, transmitted, or otherwise be copied for public or private use—other than for "fair use" as brief quotations embodied in articles and reviews without prior written permission.

Printed by BookSurge Publishing

Cover photograph by Jordon Aasland

DEDICATION

*To Kevin and Andrew—
my sons, my legacy*

Acknowledgments

Writing a book is a significant undertaking. In addition to the untold hours I've spent on the project, I've been fortunate to enjoy significant help and support from many others, all of whom have contributed to making this work better than it would have otherwise been. I sincerely appreciate the time, attention and efforts of all who have helped.

First, I must thank my wife Janet who, through her constant encouragement, keeps me in a positive state of mind. Besides her emotional support, she is always the first one to read each chapter and provide unbiased feedback as to how successful I've been in conveying my thoughts. In addition, she occasionally steps behind the camera to take some of the photographs I use to illustrate certain concepts.

My good friend Vivian Mason was instrumental in designing the book. Her professional expertise in this field is an asset that few authors enjoy, especially free of charge. She also was kind enough to edit my manuscript, saving me from potentially embarrassing grammatical errors.

Besides those who know me and may have felt obligated to help, I have received noteworthy and invaluable assistance from several people who were complete strangers at the start of this project. First, the folks at Sierra Bullets couldn't have been more cooperative in putting this book together. Early on, Matt Reams, Vice-President of Sales and Marketing, granted me permission to reproduce graphs and other data, generated from my Sierra Ballistic software program, to illustrate important truths about bullet flight. To the extent I've been successful, I doubt much of the subject matter could have been made understandable absent this consideration. Later in the process, ballistic technician Paul Box agreed to review technical aspects of the book, providing comfort that I hadn't gone astray of major scientific principles, as well as offering constructive advice.

Leupold and Stevens, through their Marketing and Communications Supervisor Patrick Mundy, gave permission to use company images and artwork that greatly enhanced the book's visual appeal and assisted in bringing the written word to life.

Finally, I'm grateful to Alan Bean for allowing me to reproduce an image of his painting, "The Hammer and the Feather." Some of you may remember that Alan went to the moon on the mission of Apollo 12. Since he left the astronaut program in 1981, he has become an accomplished artist. I will always be grateful for his kindness.

All photographs were taken by the author, unless otherwise noted.

Table of Contents

Preface	9
Introduction	13
Why We Miss	17
Let's Go Ballistic	27
Shooting Up—Shooting Down	59
Good Shooting Mechanics	83
Steady or Not	101
Mind Games & Mental Toughness	125
Effective Practice	141
Shooting in Wind	155
Long-Range Shooting	165
Shooting with Iron Sights	191
Finding the Range	215
A Few Words About Equipment	229
Glossary	235
Resources	245

PREFACE

In the eyes of many, the authorship of a book, in and of itself, bestows the mantle of expert on the writer. That's not how I feel. Although there are many well-written and informative books in publication, every profession has its phonies and frauds—hunting and writing about hunting are no different. Like most of you, over the years I've read numerous hunting books and articles. Some contain information that I have found to be unhelpful, misleading or outright false.

For the record, I don't consider myself to be either an expert shot or an expert hunter. However, I have been blessed with the time, financial resources and physical gifts to pursue what I enjoy doing most—hunt big-game animals. During my apprenticeship in the world of big-game hunting, I've continually acquired knowledge, experience and ability that would have otherwise escaped me. I've made my share of mistakes, learned some tough lessons, and made many adjustments over time. But I'm a better hunter and big-game shot now than I was just five years ago. And I hope to be better still, five years from now. And so, my observations and experiences in the real world of hunting are what I bring to this work, along with the hope that others can benefit from them.

In the sporting literature there are books about hunting big game and there are books devoted to the shooting sports. I've certainly acquired useful information from books of both genres which has helped me develop as a hunter. Unfortunately, "how-to" shooting books tend to focus on rifles, loads and technique, without incorporating information that would be useful in real-world hunting situations. At the same time, books about hunting tend to emphasize either stirring tales about particular hunts or species-specific information and recommendations, without adequate discussion about the particular challenges involved in shot preparation and execution. What's been absent, in my view, is a book written specifically for the big-game hunter, but devoted to the acquisition of relevant knowledge and the particular shooting skills required to be consistently successful in taking animals. What follows is my attempt to fill this perceived void and offer practical information and advice that interested readers can use to make themselves more proficient shots on big-game animals.

Consequently, this book is written with the following goals: provide the reader with all the information germane to shooting at big-game animals in the real world; identify the skill sets needed to consistently make shots on these animals; and offer techniques and regimens to strengthen shooting skills and eliminate weaknesses. The benefits to the reader who makes a serious attempt to follow this advice are: increased confidence when taking shots at game; the ability to make shots over ranges and under conditions which exceed one's current ability; a decrease in the number of shots that must be turned down due to their length and/or difficulty; less wounded game and more satisfying hunting experiences.

This book is not written for those who are unconcerned with repeatedly missing shots that could reasonably be expected to be made or those who handle disappointment well. Neither do I expect this work to find a large audience among those who feel that good marksmanship is primarily genetic in nature and accrues without benefit of knowledge or effort.

If, however, missing game gnaws at your soul or you find yourself turning down shots that are a little too far or too difficult for your current abilities, there's much that can be done to correct these inadequacies. If you're willing to invest time and attention towards improving your shooting capabilities, then it's my belief (and fervent hope) that what follows will be of assistance in helping you become a better, more proficient big-game shot across a wide spectrum of shooting situations, and with a variety of weapons.

This is a very nice Dall sheep I was fortunate to take in the Chugach mountains of Alaska. *Photo by Steve Johnson*

INTRODUCTION

Each year tens of thousands of North American hunters flock to woods, swamps, prairies and mountains in pursuit of their favorite big-game animals. From the nearly ubiquitous whitetail deer and black bears to the more exotic species such as caribou and wild sheep, hunters hope to place their tag on at least one of these desirable creatures each hunting season. Often, one can hunt an entire season and only get a single legitimate chance at a prey animal. Whether any individual hunter is fortunate enough to take an animal might very well depend upon his or her ability to execute that one shot, once an opportunity presents itself.

But when the moment of truth arrives, how many of us are sufficiently prepared to consistently make such a shot wherever and however it presents? Some may respond by asking, "Well, how prepared do I need to be?" My response to that query is this: How comfortable would you be living with the knowledge that you missed the animal of a lifetime not because your gun and load were inadequate, but solely because of shortcomings in your shooting ability that could have been overcome with a little extra effort on your part? I suspect some who are reading this have already been to the tortured place that a blown opportunity brings you to, and are determined to prevent similar outcomes in the future.

Fortunately, how skilled we ultimately become is determined more by the seriousness of our approach than on our initial capabilities. Those who are willing to invest significant time and effort towards their betterment as marksmen will see dividends. So, with the addition of a little more knowledge combined with a lot more shooting, all of us can expect to make meaningful gains in shooting performance.

And while it would be ideal if we connected on each and every shot we took at a big-game animal, making a humane one-shot kill, we must acknowledge that such a standard of perfection isn't attainable. All hunters, given sufficient opportunities, will miss some shots they're perfectly capable of making. I'm still haunted by a couple of my miscues! Unfortunately, we'll also wound some animals with misplaced, errant or deflected shots during the course of a hunting career. That doesn't mean we should be willing to settle for mediocre marksmanship and wounded game. Instead, each of us should strive to perform to the best of our abilities. Ultimately this ethic will result in fewer missed shots and wounded animals, a greater sense of confidence and pride in our skills, and more game in the freezer.

Because big-game hunting is conducted over diverse locations—where shooting positions and distances are rarely constant and predictable—great flexibility, versatility, and sometimes even ingenuity are required to maximize the chances for success. These facts argue for capability across the spectrum of shooting positions, distances and circumstances. Having made the pitch for developing one's shooting skills as broadly as feasible, I understand those hunters who, because of the sameness of their hunting circumstances, are comfortable with a more narrow definition of proficiency.

In any event, no matter how versatile a shot someone is (or wishes to become), there are important skills that all big-game hunters must possess. Accurately placing bullets on target demands a basic understanding of ballistics and the major external factors that can influence a bullet in flight, the various shooting positions and shooting aids that can be employed when shooting, how sighting systems can be used to best advantage, how to mentally prepare for shooting opportunities and cope with self-imposed pressure to perform, and how to maximize one's time at the practice range.

Perhaps the best place to begin an in-depth tutorial on becoming an excellent game shot is to enumerate all the reasons and explanations for failing to make good on shot opportunities. By identifying the numerous and varied things that can go wrong, we should be able to identify the necessary corrections. Along the way, we can expect to expand our knowledge base, minimize weaknesses, build confidence and become better hunters.

One of the missed shots I've accumulated over the years. In this instance, at least I know why I didn't connect.

Why We Miss

It's a given that all of us who have spent significant time hunting big game have missed a shot here or there. Despite our best intentions and efforts, an occasional off-target bullet can be expected, although not happily so. When I speak here of misplaced shots, I do so in the broadest possible sense. In this context, any shot that doesn't hit where we expect it to land can be considered to have strayed from its mark. That definition certainly includes bullets that fail to strike any part of a target animal, but it also includes shots that result in hits to unintended anatomical locales—whether or not such hits ultimately prove fatal or the animal is eventually recovered.

A common example of this last type of errant shot would be a bullet breaking an animal's backbone when the aiming point was low in the chest (heart/lung) on a broadside presentation. For most North American big-game species this discrepancy would translate into approximately twelve inches. For the largest game, such as elk and moose, this shot misplacement would be considerably greater.

Whether the bullet hit the backbone or the intended point of impact, low and just behind the front leg, may seem a trivial matter to some. After all, at least in this instance, the result would be the same—a dead animal. Many would find it easy (and preferable) to accept the outcome and congratulate themselves on a successful hunt. Of course, in other circumstances it might be quite difficult to overlook the results of a poor shot. It's pretty hard to put a happy face on an all-day, and unsuccessful, search for a gut-shot animal, for example. Becoming a truly good shot demands intellectual honesty about one's actual performance and constant curiosity as to how and why individual shots failed to find their intended mark—no matter where they may have landed. Having said that, however, there will always be occasions when a shot clearly and cleanly misses its mark, but it's nearly impossible to figure out just where the errant projectile came to rest. These instances drive me nuts! Without knowing the where, explaining the why is problematic; and without the why, confidence in subsequent shots simply evaporates.

Hitting a target with a bullet is, at the same time, both a simple proposition and a complicated task fraught with numerous opportunities for something to go wrong. It is a fact that a bullet will arrive at the desired location if a gun is aimed at the correct place and the trigger is smoothly released without disturbing that aiming point. That's the simple part. The complicated part is knowing where to point the gun given the variables of range, vertical angle, wind speed and direction, and position of the animal; holding the gun still in often uncomfortable and unsteady situations; and executing that smooth trigger release when the pressure is on.

There is much that can be done to help ensure that the vast majority of the shots we take at game animals hit reasonably close to where they are supposed to go. The first step in this process is to examine the many and diverse causes of misplaced bullets. This study will, in turn, allow us expand our knowledge, improve upon our skills and take any necessary corrective actions, so our marksmanship doesn't let us down at that crucial moment in time when we need it the most.

If it were possible to catalog all the shots on big game that have been missed, as well as the unbiased reasons for those outcomes, the vast majority of such failures would be attributed to "operator error" of one kind or another. In fact, most missed shots can be traced to failings, inadequacies, or deficiencies of knowledge that exist prior to ever stepping into the woods or mountains.

There are very few truly external influences that operate completely beyond the shooter's control. These factors include unseen obstructions which can deflect a shot, such as branches and twigs in woody environs, and unexpected animal movement just as the trigger is pulled.

Wind is another external factor which impacts bullet flight, often in difficult to predict ways, and especially at longer ranges. Although wind speed and direction are discernable, compensating for wind is often problematic, since the velocity and direction are seldom constant over the entire distance between predator and prey.

If you need to travel great distances to hunt, airline baggage handlers sometimes constitute a significant threat to your ability to hit your target, and they always detract from your peace of mind. There's nothing quite like having careless airport employees ruin all the hard work you've put into getting your gun to hit exactly where you want it to. What the airlines do with your guns is certainly beyond your control. Making sure your firearm still prints where you expect it to, once you reach your destination, is very much within your control. And you should definitely take the time to re-verify your zero before you begin the hunt—assuming your gun case actually shows up at the baggage carrousel. Of course, this same advice is equally relevant for other circumstances where your rifle may have incurred a significant jolt while hunting, such as a mishap with a horse or a hard fall where the gun whacked a rock.

The remaining factors that can adversely impact shot placement are substantially within our ability to manage—at least to some degree. That's good news, as we can make improvements and reduce deficiencies. The bad news is that there are many individual items that must be addressed to become a good shot. Almost all of these elements can be broadly characterized as issues of familiarity or preparation. Here's my list of the remaining reasons for missing, in no particular order of importance—poor shooting mechanics, unstable shooting position, unsure how uphill/downhill angles alter aiming point, lack of emotional control (buck fever), inaccurate gun/load, unknown distance to target, lack of familiarity with ballistics of chosen ammo, not knowing where animal's vitals are located, insufficient or ineffective practice, and lack of familiarity with weapon's handling (trigger pull). Next, I'll present an overview explaining the significance each of the aforementioned factors plays in getting a bullet to its target, before expanding on these topics in subsequent chapters.

Every firearm has an inherent level of precision over which we have no control. That is, each gun is capable of placing repeated shots within some proximity to all the other shots fired from the same gun with the same ammunition. We refer to this quality of repeatability as the ability to "group" shots. Depending upon what ammunition is being used, the same gun can be expected to vary in its performance, sometimes significantly. And no matter what ammunition is used, once the human element is introduced to shooting any gun/load combination, group size can be expected to expand. In order to minimize the possibility of errant shots, especially at longer ranges, it's important that we start with a reasonably precise firearm. Fortunately for consumers, many of the current out-of-the-box production guns are built to close tolerances and are capable of fine accuracy. In addition, there are several good custom and semi-custom gun makers whose products typically best those that are mass-produced.

In most hunting situations, it's not feasible to tote along

a bench rest to shoot from, so we must make do with something less than the absolute steadiness provided by a bench and sand bags. While in the field, a hunter can take a shot at a big-game animal from an array of possible shooting configurations, some of which possess more inherent stability than others. These platforms include standing, sitting, kneeling and prone. External supports or aids, such as trees, rocks, shooting sticks and slings, may or may not be available to help make a particular position more solid. Many times improvisation is required to develop the best possible shooting position for the circumstances. No matter what conditions we face, we'll all be better shots and more successful hunters if we become proficient shooting from field positions, and if we always seek the steadiest position available to us when launching bullets at game.

Some hunters feel they can go out a couple of days before the hunting season opens, shoot a handful of rounds through their favorite rifle, and presto, they're all set come opening morning. Given that kind of approach, it's going to be difficult to become a truly accomplished big-game shot. There are no shortcuts to expertise, in hunting or any other field of endeavor. Practice is necessary for proficiency, but the type of training you undertake can influence not only how skilled you eventually become, but how long it takes to gain that expertise. In order to maximize our abilities and reduce the time spent acquiring the necessary shooting skills for big-game hunting, practice regimens should be tailored to the expected task.

Proper shooting technique or mechanics must be instilled and developed or we'll never realize our full potential as shooters. The goal is to refine good shooting habits through repetition, so they eventually become second nature. The concepts of natural gun point, sight alignment, sight picture, trigger pull and follow-through, combined with proper breathing, must be ingrained. At the same time, bad habits, such as flinching, must be eliminated.

Lack of familiarity with how a gun operates can cost us game. In critical moments you shouldn't have to consciously think about where the safety is or how to quickly add rounds to the magazine, for example. The operation of such features should come automatically, seared into our brains by repeated use. Besides advancing the smooth performance of routine operational functions, practice fosters an intimate knowledge of your weapon's most important part—the trigger. Training your trigger finger to "know" just how much force can be applied and exactly when that trigger is about to break, is crucial to the gun discharging at just the right moment—when the sights are transfixed on the correct aiming point.

Shooting over level ground is a relatively simple matter, largely because understanding the relationship between gravity, the gun's sights and bullet flight is easier to visualize and comprehend in this format. However, once the gun is raised or lowered from the horizontal, aiming becomes less straightforward. Vertical shooting angles, whether positive or negative, require a more complex analysis in determining where the proper point of aim should be. Numerous articles on the subject of uphill/downhill shooting have appeared in hunting and shooting publications over the years. Unfortunately, many of these pieces have contained misleading, incomplete or, in some cases, downright inaccurate information. As a result, significant misunderstanding still exists among many hunters and shooters regarding what aiming adjustments are warranted when shooting uphill or downhill.

Not knowing how distant a target animal is from your gun barrel can be a significant impediment to proper aiming and accurate shooting, especially at longer ranges. As a bullet travels downrange from the gun's muzzle, its trajectory curve steepens. At some distance downrange, as bullet drop becomes more severe, range determination becomes critical or shots are likely to be vertically misplaced. In some instances, a ranging error of as little as twenty-five yards could spell the difference between a clean kill and a clean miss. Fortunately there are several techniques available to estimate range. And, the development of the modern portable rangefinder has made exact range determination a reality.

Anyone can go to the range, fire some shots from their favorite rifle, note where the bullets strike, and adjust the scope so the bullets hit where the shooter would like them to. When finished with such an exercise, the practitioner may say with confidence that the rifle is shooting two inches high at 100 yards, for example. That's fine, but just how useful is this information? If all subsequent shots are taken at 100 yards, then no additional data is needed. If, however, there's an expectation that shots will be taken at various other ranges, then it would be nice to know where the bullet will be at those distances, given that it's known to be two inches high at 100 yards. It just isn't acceptable to hunt game with so little information regarding bullet flight at one's disposal. What's needed is data indicating where the bullet will be relative to the line of sight across the spectrum of potential shooting distances and angles. There are two ways of acquiring such information. One way would entail shooting at representative ranges and angles, observing the results, and then cataloging them for future reference. The other method would involve taking the information already in hand (i.e., two inches high at 100 yards), and then use a ballistic software program to compute the bullet path at various other ranges and angles. This approach would require some deeper appreciation of bullet flight, as well as the necessary inputs of ballistic coefficient and muzzle velocity. In order to shoot accurately, though, it's absolutely imperative that the person manipulating the trigger know where the bullet will be relative to the sights for all shots that are contemplated.

If you expect to cleanly kill an animal you must know something about that critter's anatomy. And all animals are not put together exactly the same way. In most hunting situations the preferred final destination for bullets is the area encompassing the heart and lungs. The reason for this is threefold. Most importantly, a solid hit to this area will prove fatal, usually within a very short period of time. Second, the heart and lungs present a suitably large target, one where even a significant error in bullet placement can still result in a clean kill. Finally, very little meat is spoiled by hits to this location. I suspect most hunters already know these things, but they bear repeating. However, when you look at a particular animal, do you know where these organs are actually located in relation to other prominent anatomical features? That's a relatively simple question if we were only concerned with a broadside presentation. Even then, I suspect some would err slightly. On other presentations, especially when viewed from above or below, visualizing the whereabouts of these organs becomes more complicated. In these circumstances, many more of us would likely fail to select the correct aiming point to ensure our bullet reaches its intended target. While it's critical that we begin our hunts with a working knowledge of the anatomy of our prey species, this subject is beyond the scope of this book. For those who require more detailed information, I suggest other works dedicated solely to anatomical shot placement, such as "The Perfect Shot—North America" by Craig Boddington.

Too often, months of hard work and preparation go down the drain when we fail at that one remaining task standing between us and an animal—executing a good trigger pull. Most of the time, failing at this juncture has nothing to do with shooting mechanics and everything to do with a lack of mental or emotional control brought on by the excitement of being in proximity to our quarry or by the self-induced pressure of the moment. Lack of concentration and discipline, and a tendency to rush the shot are the manifestations of this disease we sometimes refer to as "buck fever." There are techniques we can employ, both in the field and in practice sessions, to help control the unwanted and unhelpful stresses we sometimes experience while hunting.

From a shooting perspective, I've briefly touched upon the various challenges we can be expected to face while hunting big game. Next we'll need to examine each piece of the shooting puzzle in detail, understand its importance to the larger goal of becoming a good shot, and work at perfecting that skill. And just like the childhood building blocks of old: we can take each acquired ability and add it to others to first form a steady foundation and then subsequently stack talents one on another until we eventually construct a complete and solid structure that embodies an unshakable ability to hit what we're aiming at. Now, let's get to work!

Alan Bean's painting "The Hammer and the Feather," depicting fellow astronaut Dave Scott performing an experiment regarding gravity on the surface of the moon. *Image courtesy of Alan Bean*

Let's Go Ballistic

For some hunters, just the thought of ballistics—with all the attendant physics and math—can be a painful reminder of high school days long past. But before anyone's eyes glaze over or someone decides this would be a good opportunity to put the book down and take a nap, let me explain the significance of this subject matter and relate my goals for this chapter. I believe anybody who aspires to be an accomplished shooter or hunter should possess some rudimentary understanding of what factors affect bullet flight and how they do so. At the very least, a working knowledge of ballistics will assist us in selecting equipment to match its expected task, as well as optimizing that equipment so we get the best performance possible.

It's my intent to only present subject matter that has significant and direct bearing on the sport of big-game hunting, and do this in a way that is both straightforward and understandable. This is not the place, nor I the best person, to advance an exhaustive treatise on the science of ballistics. In the interests of brevity and readability, I will omit any scientific proofs or mathematical calculations that would serve to support statements, findings or figures. Having said that, there are many relevant ballistic terms that must be defined and discussed, and the language needed to do this must be exact or confusion will ensue. Therefore, the words and phrases used to present the following material have been chosen with great care.

Finally, in order to present a tutorial that complies with my stated goals of comprehension and simplicity, I've been forced to take some small liberties with the science involved in bullet flight. These intentional oversights and corner-cutting include: ignoring minor factors affecting flight, the rounding-off of numbers and the use of approximations. In every instance, these tactics were employed to facilitate the reader's understanding of major principles and concepts. At no time was any license taken that would serve to materially misrepresent what actually happens to bullets in flight. I want everyone to see the forest and not the trees! But I encourage anyone who desires more detail to seek additional sources for a more in-depth study—and a more complete understanding—of bullet flight.

****

Ballistics is the science dealing with the motion, behavior and effects of projectiles. A projectile is any object, such as a bullet, which is given an initial velocity and which subsequently follows a path determined by the gravitational force acting on it and by the frictional resistance of the atmosphere. The study of ballistics can be separated into three distinct fields—internal, external and terminal. As it relates to firearms, internal ballistics is concerned with what transpires from the time the trigger is released until a bullet exits the barrel of a firearm. Terminal ballistics focuses on what happens once a bullet impacts a target. External ballistics, which is the focus of this chapter, concentrates on bullets while they are in flight.

When the firing pin hits the primer of a round of ammunition, a controlled explosion is initiated which results in a bullet exiting the end of the gun barrel, or muzzle, at high speed. From the moment the bullet leaves the gun two things are undeniably and universally true, at least on this planet. First, the force of gravity exerts a pull on the bullet, causing it to fall towards earth. Second, the bullet slams into the atmosphere, causing a slowing of its velocity or speed. For now, let's examine these two phenomena separately.

GRAVITY

Gravity is the principal influence acting upon a bullet in a direction perpendicular to the earth's surface. The force of gravity causes the bullet to fall or drop. Furthermore, the force of gravity causes the constant acceleration of any freely falling body, without regard to the body's size, shape or weight—at least in a vacuum. That means that any object will take the same time to fall to the ground when dropped from the exact same height. It's irrelevant whether the object is big or small, heavy or light, or how it's shaped; they will all hit the ground simultaneously. Some of you may remember seeing Dave Scott on the surface of the moon during the mission of Apollo 15. He simultaneously dropped a feather and a hammer, both of which hit the moon's surface at the same instant, giving visual testament to this important truth about gravity.

As I stated previously, the acceleration of a free-falling object caused by the force of gravity is constant, at least in a vacuum. As you are all aware, we are surrounded by an atmosphere. However, it can be shown that the effect of air resistance on bullet drop over short vertical distances is negligible. That means the presence of our atmosphere can be practically ignored when discussing gravity's effect on bullets. Therefore, the acceleration of a bullet (at or near the earth's surface) can be assumed to be the same as that in a vacuum, which can be calculated to be approximately 32 feet/second^2. And knowing this, a bullet's drop in relation to the central axis of the barrel can be calculated solely as a function of time. Furthermore, every bullet, regardless of the bullet's weight, shape or form, will have dropped the same distance at any given time.

Some of you are probably wondering, "That's fine for bullets we drop by hand, but doesn't a bullet's speed help slow how fast it drops?" The answer is emphatically no! It's difficult for some to comprehend that how far a bullet (any bullet) drops has nothing to do with how fast it begins its journey in a horizontal direction. The effects of gravity operate completely independent of a bullet's horizontal velocity. How far a bullet falls is, therefore, strictly a function of the time gravity has to act upon that bullet. Consequently, we can calculate a bullet's position relative to the muzzle, in a direction perpendicular to the earth (drop), if we know how long it's been in flight. Conversely, we can calculate how long a bullet has been in flight if we know how far it's dropped in relation to the gun's muzzle.

AIR RESISTANCE

We've seen that gravity is the main force influencing the vertical component of bullet flight. The horizontal or down-range component of bullet flight is primarily affected by the denseness of the surrounding air. The impediment to bullet flight caused by air is a force known as aerodynamic drag. A bullet fired in a vacuum will leave the muzzle with a certain velocity, and maintain that velocity for as long as the bullet's in flight. By contrast, a bullet fired into the atmosphere will immediately begin to lose velocity once it exits the barrel. Some bullets are less affected by air resistance, or exhibit less drag, than do others.

How rapidly any particular bullet loses its velocity is very much a function of its design. As you might expect, long, slender pointed bullets tend to slice through air more efficiently than do short, stocky blunt-nosed bullets. One measure of a bullet's ability to resist air pressure is known as its ballistic coefficient. The higher the ballistic coefficient of a given bullet, the less drag it has and the more efficiently it travels through air. Of particular import for hunters is the fact that bullets with high ballistic coefficients retain higher down-range velocities (and therefore energies), have flatter trajectories and exhibit less drift caused by wind, than do their less-efficient counterparts.

Just as gravity works independently of horizontal velocity in determining how far a bullet drops from the muzzle in a direction perpendicular to the earth's surface, the distance a bullet travels downrange is independent of gravity—at least theoretically. As a practical matter, most fired bullets will hit the ground before their horizontal velocity becomes zero. When that happens, gravity could be said to have acted long enough so as to prevent further horizontal flight. So in this narrow sense, gravity is relevant to the distance a bullet travels downrange. Otherwise, the magnitude of the horizontal component of a bullet's flight is dependent on its initial velocity and by its ability to combat air resistance.

BULLET FLIGHT ON LEVEL GROUND

So far, we've identified the two main external factors affecting bullet flight—gravity and the atmosphere—and independently detailed their effects on bullets in flight. Let's do some shooting and see what happens when both factors are operating on a bullet at the same time. On this occasion, I'm going to put a rifle into a special shooting rest with an integral vice, place a carpenter's level on the barrel and adjust the barrel until the long axis is level with the ground, then tighten the vise. The barrel is three feet from the ground. Next, I'm going to chamber a round of ammunition and shoot. What can we expect to observe?

First, no matter the caliber of the rifle, the weight of the bullet or its shape, or the muzzle velocity of the bullet, we can expect each and every bullet fired to take the same amount of time to hit the ground. Actually, we can be more specific than that. By using some fairly simple math we can determine that it will take approximately .45 seconds for our bullet, or any object, to fall to the ground from an elevation of three feet. That means that any bullet we fire from this particular set-up will only be in the air for .45 seconds. How far a particular bullet travels downrange during that brief period of time depends on two entirely different things: how fast the bullet is traveling as it starts its journey, and how efficiently the bullet slices through the air.

So in order to continue our study, we'll need additional information about any ammunition we fire. If we are provided the muzzle velocity and ballistic coefficient of each bullet, we should be able to calculate the horizontal distance any bullet travels in .45 seconds (or any interval of time, for that matter).

I own a rifle chambered in .30-06, so let's shoot that first, but with two different loads. For this first experiment I want the only variable to be the ballistic coefficient. Therefore, I load both rounds with Speer® bullets weighing 150 grains each and identical powder charges. Both rounds leave the muzzle with the exact same velocity—2,800 feet per second (fps). The only difference between the two cartridges is the shape of the bullets. The first bullet is pointed and has a boat-tail base. These features help account for the bullet's fairly high ballistic coefficient of .423. Calculations show this bullet will travel about 362 yards during the .45 seconds it is aloft.

The second bullet has a ballistic coefficient of only .266, mainly because it has a blunt round nose. When I perform similar calculations for this second bullet, I find it only travels 334 yards before striking the ground. Obviously, the bullet with the more efficient design traveled farther before hitting the ground. This is because the pointed bullet was able to retain more velocity than the round-nosed bullet. In fact, when the pointed bullet hits the ground its speed is 2,070 feet per second (fps). By comparison, the velocity of the round-nosed bullet is only 1,771 fps when it comes to rest (See Table 1).

TABLE 1—COMPARATIVE VELOCITIES (fps)		
Time (seconds)	**A**	**B**
0	2,800	2,800
.10	2,606	2,502
.20	2,433	2,250
.30	2,277	2,036
.40	2,136	1,854
.45	2,070	1,771

A-Speer .308 150 grain boat-tail, B.C.=.423
B-Speer .308 150 grain round nose, B.C.=.266

We've already demonstrated that the distance any bullet drops is solely a function of the length of time the force of gravity is allowed to act on that bullet. In other words, each unit of time (seconds) corresponds to a specific amount of drop (inches), and vice versa. I initially chose to describe bullet drop in terms of elapsed time to show the important relationship between gravity and time. Since there's a direct correlation between time and bullet drop, let's look at our last experiment from a perspective more useful to hunters—bullet drop as compared to the bullet's horizontal distance from the muzzle.

If we go back to my .30-06 and the same two 150 grain Speer® bullets and plot their positions in terms of distance downrange versus drop, we'll discover that the path of each bullet is curved. (Of course, these paths would look similar if I had plotted distance versus time.) If we compare the paths of the individual bullets, we can see that the bullet with the higher ballistic coefficient will have dropped less at any given range (See Graph 1). This disparity becomes more pronounced as range increases. I've arbitrarily chosen 400 yards for the upper limit of range, in order to provide a chart that's easier to read.

When we did our initial analysis of these two .30-06 rounds, we limited how long the bullets would be in flight (time it takes to drop three feet), and measured how far they would travel in a set amount of time. In the second investigation, we removed any constraint of time, and simply plotted bullet drop versus distance traveled downrange. Nonetheless, the results are completely consistent and reconcilable. If you look at Graph 1 and focus on the positions of the bullets approximately 362 yards from the muzzle, you'll notice that the round-nosed bullet will have dropped more at that distance than will the bullet with the higher ballistic coefficient. In the first study, the same bullet traveled 28 yards less than the bullet sporting the higher ballistic coefficient. The explanation is straightforward: Once time is removed as a constraint, it takes the round-nosed bullet more time, as measured in drop, to reach the same point downrange.

To sum it all up, this experiment demonstrates that bullets that differ in their ballistic coefficients but are otherwise identical regarding caliber, weight and muzzle velocity, will exhibit different paths through the air during flight. And since the more efficient bullet (higher ballistic coefficient) drops less at every point downrange, its path can be described as "flatter" when compared to a bullet sporting a lower ballistic coefficient.

Let's do some more shooting from the same rest and vice. This time, we're going to shoot two guns of different caliber and see what happens. In the first gun, .243 Winchester in caliber, I'm going to fire a Speer® spitzer bullet weighing 90 grains at a muzzle velocity of 2,900 fps. We'll use the .30-06 again, this time utilizing a Nosler® Partition™ bul-

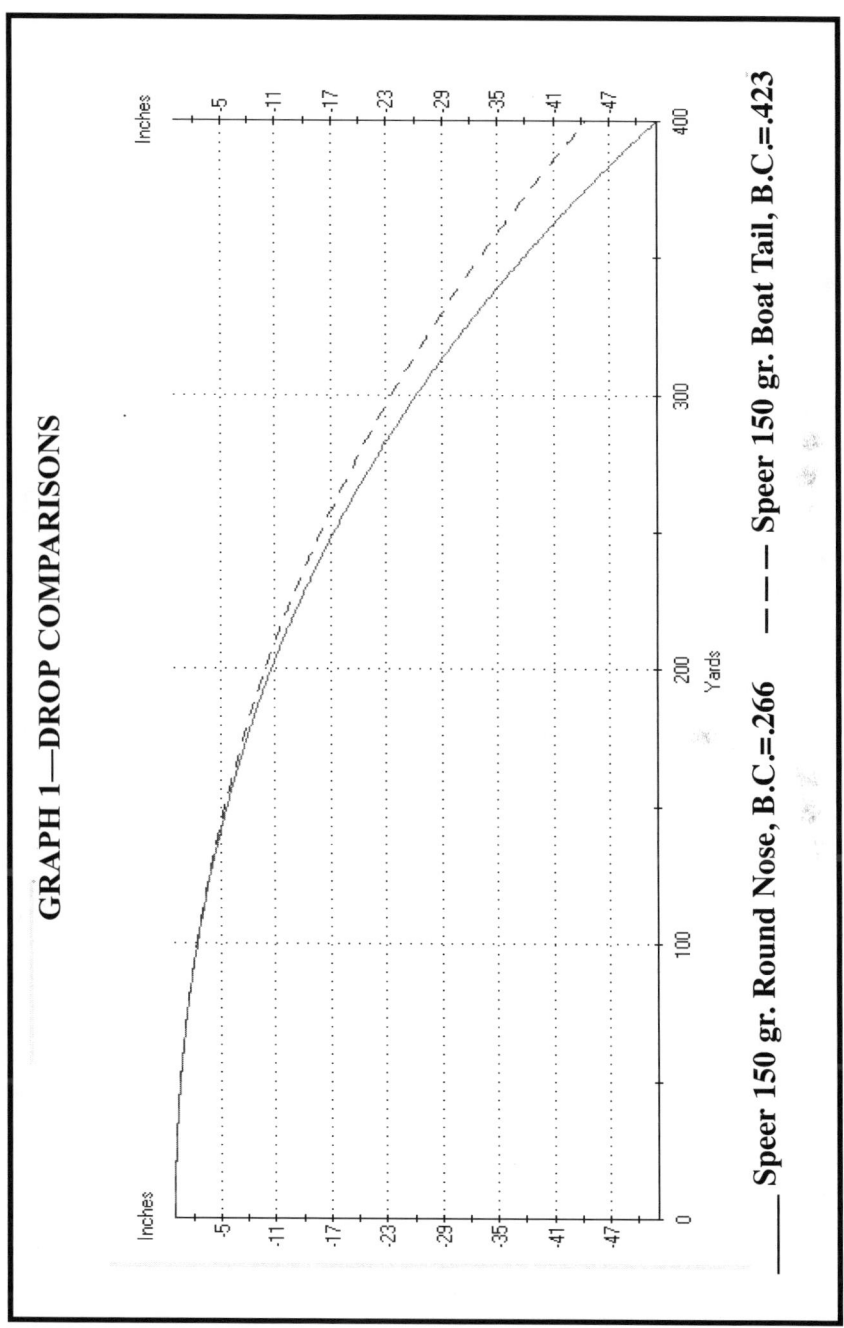

let weighing 150 grains, with an initial velocity identical to the .243 round—2,900 fps. The ballistic coefficient for both bullets is .386. Lo and behold, calculations show that both bullets hit the ground the same distance from the target—369 yards. Not unexpectedly, we also find that both bullets retain a velocity of 2,076 fps when they fall to earth .45 seconds after leaving the barrel. And, if we plot drop in terms of distance downrange for these two rounds of different caliber and bullet weight, we find that they have identical paths through the air (See Graph 2). From this experiment, we correctly conclude that bullets of different calibers and weights will, nonetheless, travel the same course if they share the same muzzle velocities and ballistic coefficients.

The path of a projectile through the air is referred to as its trajectory. Clearly, a bullet becomes a projectile when it exits the barrel of a gun, no matter its initial speed. A bullet's position anywhere along its trajectory can be calculated, assuming we know its muzzle velocity and ballistic coefficient. In general, if you were to examine the shape of a bullet's trajectory you would notice a couple of things. First, the trajectory is curved rather than linear. Second, the curve becomes increasingly more pronounced as the bullet travels further from the gun's muzzle. Thus, bullet trajectory can be described as parabolic in shape. Finally, bullets with high ballistic coefficients have trajectories that curve less dramatically than do bullets with lower ballistic coefficients. This phenomenon lends credence to the description that an efficient bullet has a flatter trajectory than a comparatively inefficient bullet.

USING TRAJECTORY TO ASSIST AIMING

Now that we understand the basic concepts of gravity, time and ballistic coefficient as they relate to bullet flight, let's advance towards real-world shooting. I purposely didn't mention sights in our previous experiments, because they

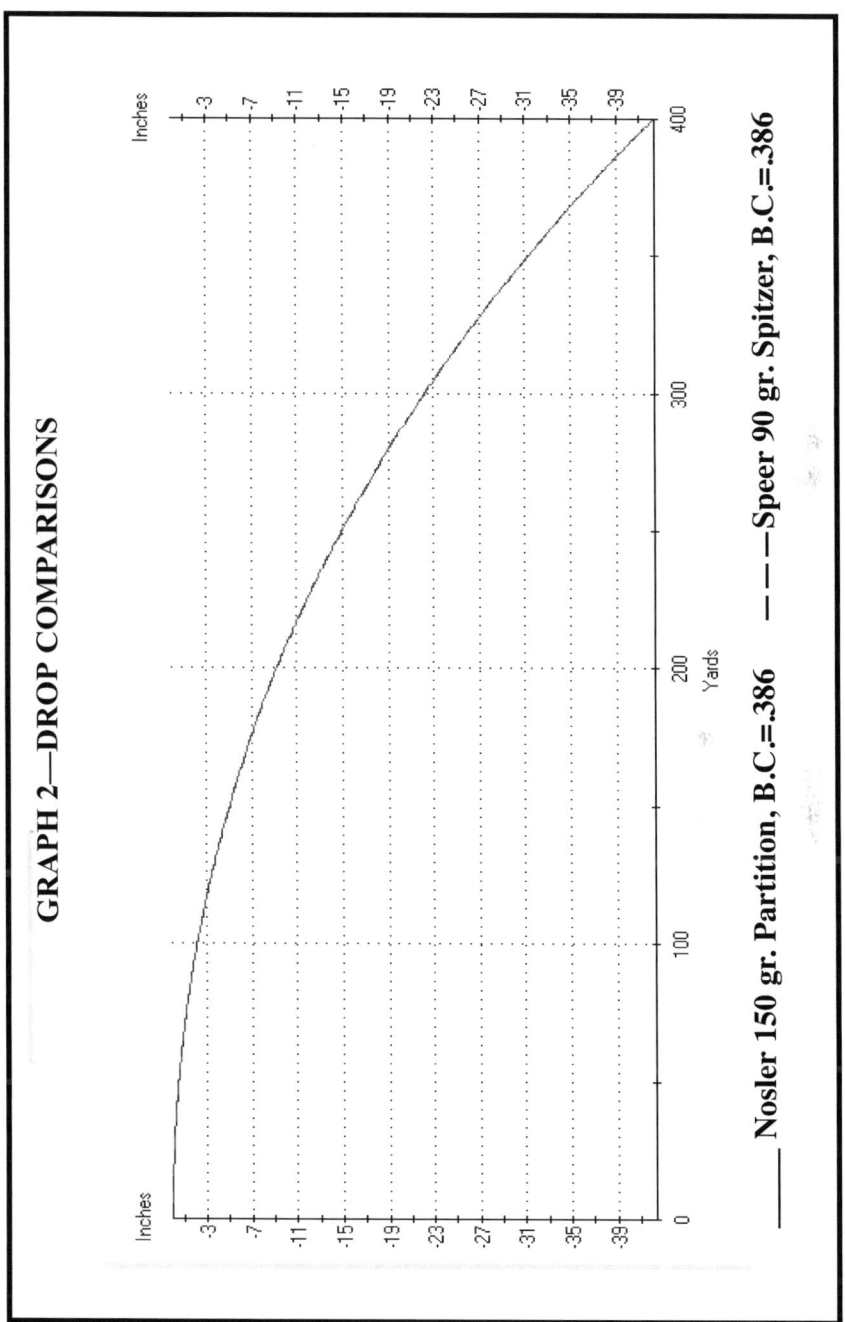

were irrelevant to a presentation of the concepts I was trying to emphasize. However, we're ultimately going to need some mechanism to aim any gun we shoot, so let's install some sights. I don't want to discuss scopes yet, so for now, we'll install front and rear iron sights. For illustration purposes, we'll assume that once the installation is complete the two sights, collectively, are aligned in an orientation perfectly parallel to the barrel and they sit one inch above the central axis of the barrel's bore. We're still using my rest and vice to shoot from, and we're going to duplicate the same shooting conditions we used in the prior tests. That means the barrel will be perfectly level and sit three feet from the ground. In addition, we'll place a suitable target 400 yards away and center it in the sights. For this experiment, I've selected my .30-06 using the Speer® boat-tail bullet weighing 150 grains, which leaves the muzzle at 2,800 fps. You may remember this bullet has a ballistic coefficient of .423. You may also remember that the last time we shot this combination, the bullet was in the air .45 seconds; and when it struck the ground, it did so 362 yards from the muzzle. When the trigger is pulled this time, what happens? And, is there any difference from the first go-around?

    In order to answer these questions, it would be helpful to examine the situation from behind the gun, just as you would if you were actually doing the shooting. When you sit down and look through the sights you see a perfectly centered target. This is your line of sight. But the line of sight is not the barrel! Remember, the center of the barrel is one inch below the sights. Therefore, the line of sight is 37 inches above the ground, not the 36-inch height the bore was set to. When the round is fired the bullet will fly exactly as it did previously. The trajectory will be the same, as will the terminal velocity (2,070 fps). The bullet will even hit the ground in the same spot—362 yards from the muzzle—because the gun is in the exact same position it was the first time we used it.

But from the shooter's perspective, the bullet will appear to have dropped 37 inches.

Since they must necessarily be mounted some distance above the bore, the introduction of sights creates an issue of perspective to bullet flight. Thus, we can view a bullet's position relative to the line of sight of the shooter, or we can address bullet flight in relation to the ground, which is the more absolute comparison. It may be to our advantage to adopt one perspective for one analysis, and the other vantage point for a different study. For the majority of occasions, viewing bullet flight in relation to the shooter's line of sight is the more helpful perspective. What's really important is that everyone understands that line of sight and barrel bore are not one and the same.

If we return to our last shooting set-up, we can calculate where our bullet would be at 100-yard increments relative to the line of sight (LOS). We would find the bullet to be approximately 3.5 inches below the LOS at 100 yards, 11.0 inches below the LOS at 200 yards and 24.6 inches below the LOS at 300 yards. We could use this information to aim our gun at game while hunting. For example, in order to hit an animal standing 200 yards away, we would point the sights 11 inches above the intended impact point. But by adopting this method, we would need to aim high by a specific—and different—allotment for each shot, depending on the range. This approach is fraught with problems. I'm sure this method doesn't strike any of you as being particularly worthy in real-life hunting situations. We can definitely do better.

To optimize our ability to aim at, and hit, game at distance we can manipulate the sights as they relate to the bore. If you remember, in our last shooting scenario the line of sight and the bore were intentionally kept parallel. By making minor adjustments to the sights we can cause the line of sight and the line of the bore to intersect. This approach will provide advantages, as we'll shortly see.

The actual adjustments will be made to the sights, whether open or telescopic. However, conceptually, it's quite valid to view the effect as one of elevating the barrel so the line of the bore intersects the line of sight. Most people find that by adopting this convention it's easier to visualize what's going on. In fact, when we step back and look at the bigger picture, we are actually elevating the bore above the horizontal, if ever so slightly. At the same time, the line of sight remains level with the ground, at least until we discuss shooting at vertical angles.

Now that we've altered the sights so that the line of sight and the bore line intersect, let's examine what will happen when a bullet is fired from our gun. When it leaves the muzzle, the bullet is below the line of sight. But, at some point downrange the bullet will cross the line of sight. The bullet will then travel some distance while above the line of sight. At some range the bullet will cross the line of sight a second time. The remainder of the bullet's flight will be below the line of sight.

The previous paragraph described the bullet's path from the perspective of the shooter's line of sight. It's important to understand that bullet flight in relation to the bore of the barrel has not changed, however. Just because we elevated the barrel somewhat, none of the laws of physics have been suspended. From the moment the bullet exits the barrel, the force of gravity is working to pull the bullet earthward, and it drops continuously with constant acceleration, just as before. At no time does the bullet actually rise above the bore line!

The second intersection between bullet and line of sight is usually described in terms of distance from the shooter, and is referred to as the range at which the gun is "zeroed-in." The good news is that we can "zero" our guns to any range we find most useful by simply adjusting the sights. For some applications we might find a 100-yard zero ideal, while in other situations a 300-yard zero might be more advantageous. The first intersection between the line of sight and the bullet occurs much closer to the muzzle. The exact location is very much dependent on what distance the rifle is zeroed to and how high above the bore the sights are mounted. For center-fire rifles sporting scopes and zeroed to 200 yards, this intersection would occur at about 25 yards for most ammunition. This information can be helpful when initially zeroing or sighting-in a rifle.

By elevating the bore in relation to the line of sight, we've constructed a much more useful tool by which to aim our guns. By using this method aiming has been greatly simplified, and we have the latitude to make further refinements to meet specific goals. Let me elaborate. To begin, we'll go back to my .30-06, on which I'll mount a scope where the center of the scope's reticle is 1.5 inches above the center of the bore. I'll still be shooting the same ammo I used earlier—the 150 grain Speer® boat-tail bullet started at 2,800 fps. I'm going to shoot this combination until I'm satisfied it's shooting "dead on" at 200 yards, and then examine where the bullet is in relation to the line of sight at various distances. Not surprisingly, I find the bullet leaves the muzzle 1.5 inches below the line of sight (LOS). At 30 yards the bullet first intersects the LOS. From 31 to 199 yards the bullet travels above the LOS. The second intersection of bullet and LOS occurs at the 200-yard mark, as per design. Starting at 201 yards, and for the rest of its flight, the bullet is once again below the LOS. Of even more significance to us as hunters is this fact: from the time the bullet leaves the muzzle until it reaches the 260-yard mark, it's never more than four inches above or below the LOS (See Graph 3).

This is important because the heart/lung area of most big-game animals is significantly larger than four inches in diameter. Using our present example, if we were to aim for the center of these organs, the bullet should strike no more

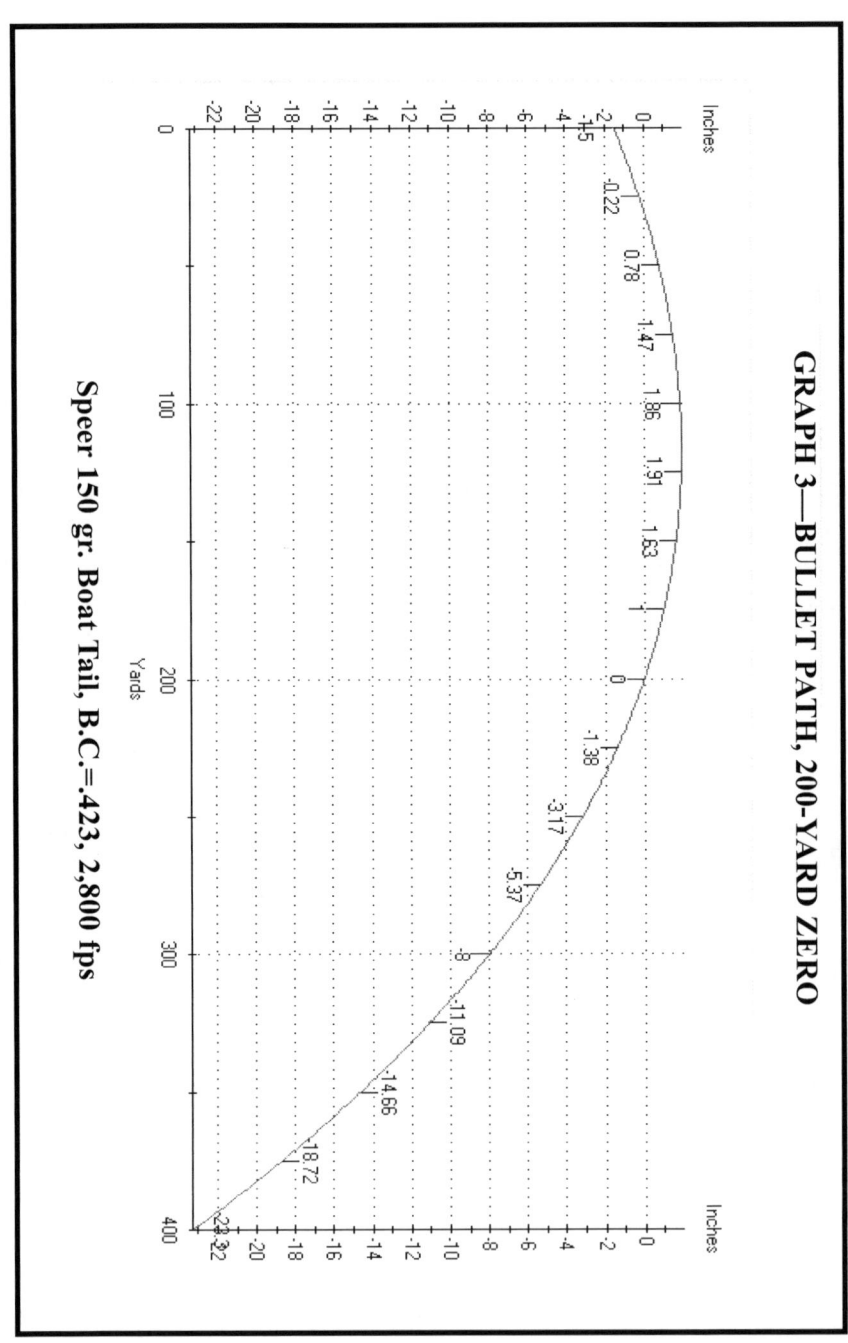

GRAPH 3—BULLET PATH, 200-YARD ZERO

Speer 150 gr. Boat Tail, B.C.=.423, 2,800 fps

than four inches high or four inches low for any range up to 260 yards, assuming good execution. That means we would make a killing shot on an animal positioned up to 260 yards away, by simply centering the sights on the vitals. And just as important, the vitals are large enough that errors in addition to this four-inch allowance could be accommodated and still result in a clean kill. We need this additional pad for things like the gun's inherent imprecision and errors attributable to the shooter, which might act to amplify any error caused by our aiming technique. Obviously, the larger the animal, the greater our cushion for accumulated error will be.

The main benefit derived from using such an approach to aiming is: no field calculations are involved, and there is no need to hold "over" (or under) the animal at these ranges. There's a shooting term that applies to this concept. The term is "point-blank" range, and it refers to targets that are sufficiently close that there is no need to consider the bullet's actual position relative to the shooter's line of sight when shooting.

Another term closely associated with the line of sight (LOS) is mid-range trajectory. This refers to the point in a bullet's flight where it is at its maximum distance above the LOS. By necessity, this occurs at some distance between the bullet's first and second intersections with the LOS, when the bullet is above the LOS. For our .30-06 with its current zero, the mid-range trajectory occurs at 120 yards, where the bullet is 1.93 inches above the LOS.

OPTIMIZING MID-RANGE TRAJECTORY

We arbitrarily chose a 200-yard zero for our analysis. But, what difference would a 250-yard zero make, and would that help or harm our ability to take game? To find out, we'll use the exact same gun and ammunition, change the zero to 250 yards, and crank out the numbers. As in the previous case, the bullet is initially 1.50 inches below the LOS. At 23 yards it crosses the LOS for the first time. The zero is 250 yards, and at 299 yards the bullet is 4.0 inches below the LOS. The mid-range trajectory occurs at 140 yards, where the bullet is 3.56 inches above the LOS (See Graph 4). Assuming a tolerance of four inches is acceptable for the game we're hunting, we discover the point-blank range has been extended from 260 yards to nearly 300 yards, simply by changing the zero from 200 to 250 yards. In other words, we've made better use of the "acceptable" error that the concept of point-blank range affords us, by balancing this error on the sight-in point.

If you recall, with the rifle zeroed at 200 yards the mid-range trajectory occurred at 120 yards, where the bullet was 1.93 inches above the LOS. This same bullet was 4.0 inches below the LOS at 260 yards. Clearly, 1.93 inches above LOS and 4.0 inches below LOS aren't well-balanced at the zero point. When sighted to 250 yards, however, the bullet is 3.56 inches above the LOS at its maximum and 4.0 inches below the LOS at 299 yards. This results in much better—but not perfect—balance about the zero (3.56 inches above LOS to 4.0 inches below LOS). Figure 1 illustrates these relationships.

We could tinker with our gun's zero until we made the maximum use of whatever error we deemed as acceptable, essentially balancing that error equally on both sides of our zero. Just keep in mind that "giving away" four inches may be too much, especially on animals with smaller vital zones and/or when using imprecise equipment. I used the four-inch convention for illustration, and it's certainly realistic for many hunting situations. The biggest concern when using this approach is one of shooting too high (and possibly over) on an animal located at or near the mid-range trajectory point. To lessen that possibility, especially on smaller animals, it may be wise to set the maximum mid-range trajectory at three inches. Of course, doing so will serve to reduce the point-blank range as well.

45

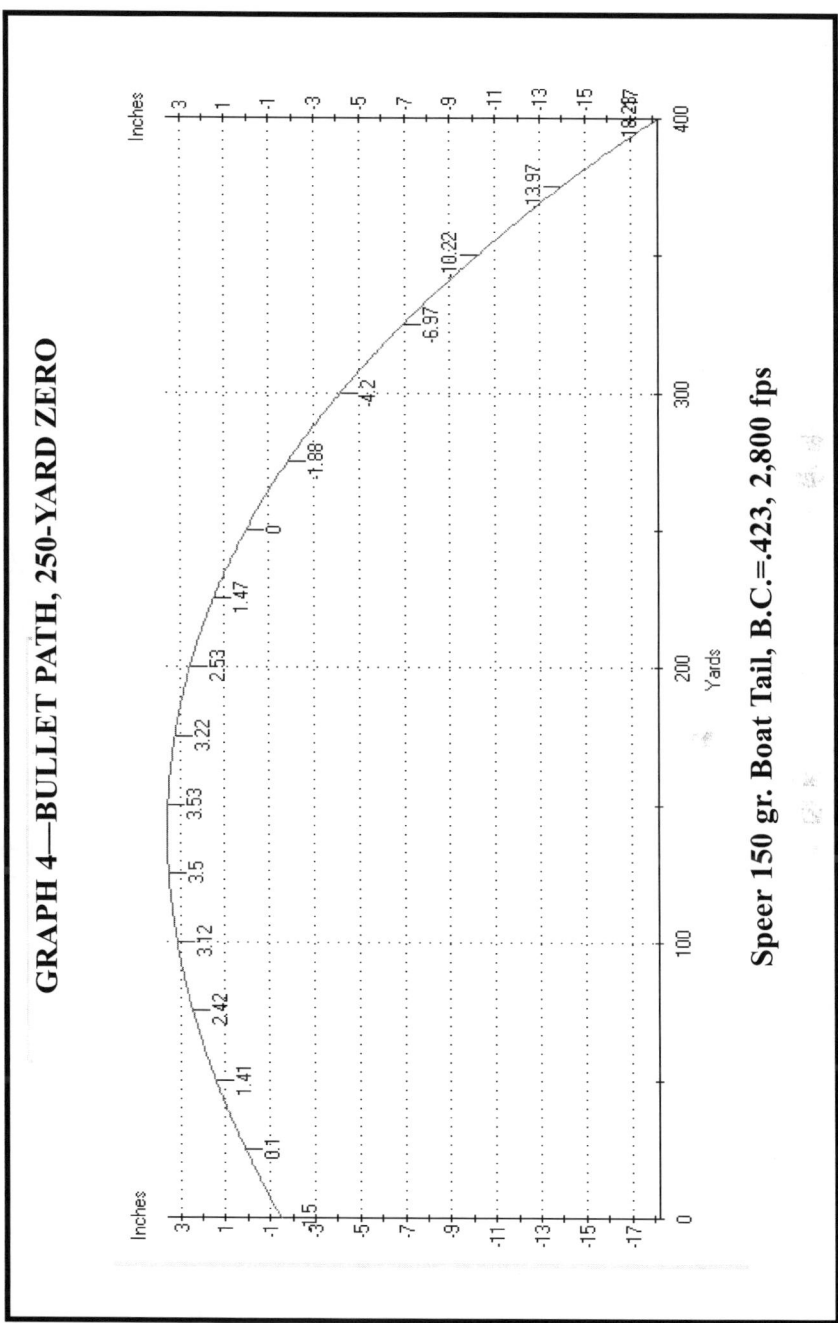

Remember, the purpose of all this is to provide ourselves with a tool that simplifies aiming our gun over the greatest possible circumstances. As such, any use of a cartridge's trajectory, as it relates to sight-in range, should be tailored with an eye towards the intended game animals and the ranges at which they can expect to be encountered. And no matter what mid-range trajectory is deemed acceptable, it will eventually be necessary to resort to some alternate means to aim, once a shot exceeds the point-blank range.

In general, if you operate on the premise that most big-game animals can accommodate an acceptable aiming error of four inches, most big-game cartridges can be sighted to hit approximately three inches high at 100 yards. Doing so will cause the rifle to hit "dead on" somewhere around 250 yards, provide a point-blank range of about 300 yards, and stay within the acceptable mid-range trajectory target of four inches.

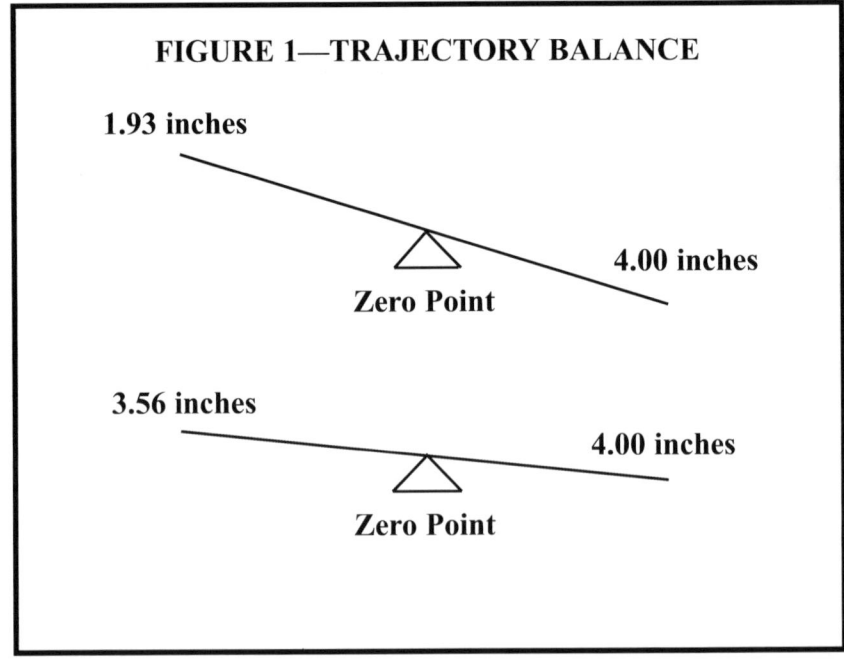

MINOR FACTORS AFFECTING BULLET FLIGHT

There are several additional and relatively minor factors which affect a bullet's flight through air. To this point I've avoided their discussion, in order to keep the presentation simple and understandable. Even now, I intend to address only the most germane influences, briefly describing their impacts on bullet flight. When appropriate, I'll also point out circumstances where these factors could escalate in importance sufficient enough to present a practical concern for a hunter in the field. Fortunately, most of the time these factors don't reach that threshold—that's why they are considered minor.

As we've seen, bullets are affected by the air they travel through. But, is it fair to say that air is the same wherever it's encountered? Well, not really. There are several environmental influences that help determine just how dense the air is in any given location. As you might expect, dense air presents more of an impediment to bullet flight than does "thin" air.

Generally speaking, air close to the earth's surface is denser than air at high altitude. The same conclusion can be made when comparing other variables related to our atmosphere. Thus, air in an area of high barometric pressure is denser than air where the barometric pressure is low; cold air is denser than warm air; and dry air is denser than moist air. Most of the time the conditions that would tend to make air dense don't all line up on the same side of the equation. For instance, at higher altitude where the air is thinner, it's usually cold. The relative denseness of cold air tends to balance somewhat the thin air found at higher altitude.

Trouble can arise when someone does the bulk of their shooting in a location that is at one extreme of air density, and they then go hunting some place where the opposite extreme of air density is common. An example of this type of scenario would be a hunter who lives and shoots near sea level, but come fall he'll be hunting at 13,000 feet. Let's see what practical effect this change in locations would make for our hypothetical hunter. We'll give the hunter a .30-06 rifle, shooting a Speer® 165 grain spitzer bullet at a muzzle velocity of 2,900 feet per second. A scope is mounted 1.5 inches above the center of the bore and the rifle is zeroed at 250 yards when he shoots at home and the temperature is 59 degrees Fahrenheit. Under these conditions we find the bullet will hit dead on at 250 yards, four inches low at 300 yards, and 17 inches low at 400 yards. Now, let's change the temperature and elevation to match the expected hunting conditions, keeping all other variables equal, and see just what differences in bullet flight our hunter can expect when he pulls the trigger at higher altitude and colder temperatures.

In general, because the air is thinner at high altitude, a bullet will meet with less air resistance. Therefore, we would expect the bullet to better retain its velocity over time. This, in turn, should cause a flattening of bullet trajectory, resulting in bullets hitting higher at a given range than would be expected in air of higher density. Indeed, at 13,000 feet and 10 degrees Fahrenheit, we find the rifle which was sighted-in at 250 yards at sea level is now shooting nearly one inch high at this same distance. At 300 yards the bullet hits three inches low, and at 400 yards the bullet strikes only 13 inches low (See Table 2).

By comparing the trajectories of the same bullet fired in two environmental extremes we can form some conclusions. First, the differences in trajectory become more pronounced as range increases. Second, as a practical matter, a hunter could ignore the effects caused by this particular change in location for any shots inside of 300 yards, as there's no more than a one-inch discrepancy in where the bullet will hit anywhere along this path. However, the situation gets increasingly dicey starting at 400 yards, where the bullet fired at altitude will hit more than three inches higher than if shot at sea

TABLE 2—COMPARATIVE BULLET PATHS (inches)

Range (yards)	Sea Level, 59°F	13,000 feet, 10°F	Difference
0	-1.50	-1.50	0
50	1.22	1.22	0.01
100	2.82	2.87	0.04
150	3.22	3.37	0.15
200	2.32	2.67	0.36
250	0.00	0.72	0.72
300	-3.85	-2.55	1.30
350	-9.36	-7.21	2.15
400	-16.68	-13.33	3.35
450	-25.97	-20.99	4.98
500	-37.41	-30.26	7.15
550	-51.21	-41.25	9.96
600	-67.58	-54.02	13.56

Speer 165 grain Spitzer, Muzzle Velocity = 2,900 fps

level. That's enough to miss an animal if a hunter is ignorant of the natural differences in air density that exist on earth, and how bullet flight can be affected by these differences. But having said all that, you can see that for most hunters, those who expect to take shots over reasonable ranges and in less disparate conditions, little consideration need be given to adjusting aim when swapping locations from home to most hunting destinations.

Earlier in this chapter, I stated that a bullet's muzzle velocity and ballistic coefficient helped determine its trajectory. At that time, we compared two bullets that weighed the same and had the same initial velocities, but different ballistic coefficients. We discovered that the bullet with the higher ballistic coefficient retained more velocity at a given range, flew farther over a given time span, and dropped less at a given distance than did its less-efficient competitor. What we didn't investigate was the effects of altering muzzle velocity on bullet flight.

Those who buy factory ammunition don't have the ability to tinker with muzzle velocity. Indeed, it is hoped (and expected) that lot-to-lot uniformity exists with whatever brand of ammunition is being used, as ammo is often purchased in different locations and months apart. Those of us who hand-load our own ammo from their individual components, however, do have the ability to adjust powder charges, and therefore velocity, while using the same bullet. But, how much actual latitude is there to alter powder charges, and how much of an impact on bullet flight can such adjustments be expected to make?

For most ammo, due to limitations of case capacity and internal pressures, the maximum practical flexibility in muzzle velocity for a given round is in the order of 200 feet per second. In addition to this constraint, it's a scientific fact that increasing muzzle velocity also increases bullet drag, so any benefit derived from stepped-up velocity is partially offset by higher air resistance. Let's perform another experiment to demonstrate the practical effects of altering muzzle velocity.

For this study we're going to shoot the same 165 grain bullet we used in the air-density experiment, but in one instance we'll achieve a muzzle velocity of 2,900 feet per second (fps), and in the second try we'll start the bullet at 2,800 fps. The resulting comparisons in bullet drop for the two rounds are shown in Table 3. As you can see, even at 400 yards the difference is only three inches. And for shorter ranges, a 100-fps increase in muzzle velocity provides a negligible advantage in regards to flattening trajectory.

The presence of our atmosphere combined with the spin imparted on a bullet by a gun's rifling results in additional forces on bullets that don't exist in a vacuum. Some of these forces act to counter the force of gravity, if ever so slightly. In a vacuum, if you were to drop an object (any object), or shoot a bullet (any bullet) from a gun where the barrel is perfectly level, all would hit the ground at the same time. How long it would take for these objects to reach the ground would depend solely on the height from which they were dropped. If released from a distance of five feet, they all would take .559 seconds to hit the dirt.

However, surrounded by air, bullets in flight receive some lift that retards the pull of gravity. Just how much lift a particular bullet enjoys is a function of several factors, including the bullet's physical characteristics, such as its form, center of gravity, and center of pressure. This is all very complicated, but bullets traveling in the presence of air will take slightly longer to fall the same distance as those dropped (or shot) in a vacuum. The actual drop times vary from bullet to bullet and they can be precisely calculated taking into account all relevant factors. By way of comparison, Table 4 shows the time it takes for several different bullets to drop five feet. As you can see, the deviations from what would occur in a vacuum are measured in a few hundredths

TABLE 3—DROP COMPARISONS (inches)

Range (yards)	A	B
100	-2.17	-2.33
150	-5.03	-5.40
200	-9.18	-9.86
250	-14.74	-15.85
300	-21.84	-23.48
350	-30.60	-32.92
400	-41.17	-44.31

A-Speer 165 grain spitzer@2,900 fps
B-Speer 165 grain spitzer@2,800 fps

TABLE 4—TIME TO DROP 5 FEET (seconds)

Any bullet (vacuum)	.559
.224 Nosler 69 gr. HP/BT@3,000fps	.608
.243 Sierra 90 gr. FMJ/BT@3,000fps	.599
.308 Speer 150 gr. Round nose@2,800fps	.612
.308 Speer 200 gr. Spitzer@2,900fps	.586
.375 Federal 300 gr. Bear Claw@2,450fps	.598
.458 Hornady 500 gr. Round nose@2,200fps	.602

of a second, which doesn't rise to the level of significance for most big-game hunters.

BALLISTICS SOFTWARE

Throughout this chapter I've supplied a great many numerical figures for things like time of flight, velocity, ballistic coefficient, mid-range trajectory and the like. I've also intimated that these values had been calculated—which is true. What I failed to explain at the time was exactly how these numbers were arrived at. For the most part, instead of doing the math myself, I obtained these values from a ballistics software computer program. Specifically, I use the Sierra® Infinity Five software, version 5.1, produced by Sierra® Bullets. There are similar products manufactured by other companies, such as Barnes Bullets®.

Although I believe many products of the computer-driven age we live in are of dubious value, I find ballistic software to be an invaluable resource for any serious shooter, hand-loader or hunter. These tools are powerful aids and provide tremendous versatility in examining and understanding bullet flight. By entering known or expected data, such as the height of the sights, elevation angle, zero and the muzzle velocity and the ballistic coefficient of a given bullet, the trajectory can be studied in terms of bullet drop and the path of the bullet relative to the line of sight over any maximum or incremental range desired. Remaining velocities and energies, as well as elapsed time of flight, are given at all ranges. Environmental factors, such as barometric pressure, altitude, temperature and wind direction and speed, can be altered from their default settings to provide accurate data over a wide spectrum of conditions. Data can be viewed in both table and graph forms.

Point-blank range can be derived by limiting "acceptable" error (i.e., vital zone) and calculating for maximum, or by limiting "acceptable" error and selecting a zero. In addition, a convenient range (e.g., 100 yards) can be entered, along with a bullet's position at that range (e.g., 3″ high), and the program will specify the distance at which the gun is sighted-in. These are valuable capabilities to have when deciding the best distance at which to zero a rifle and in verifying that the gun continues to hold its zero.

Maybe the most useful feature of ballistic software programs is the ability to make comparisons between two sets of inputs. We might want to compare two different bullets holding other variables equal. Or, it may be advantageous to study the same bullet while other variables, such as muzzle velocity, zero or sight height, are altered.

All these features give hunters tremendous capability, and without the need to set foot on a shooting range. Ballistic programs allow us to experiment with different rounds, make comparisons, formulate judgments about what we see, and make adjustments to our equipment that will benefit our ability to kill game when hunting. Best of all, ballistic software can provide accurate and useful information that will benefit any hunter or shooter, whether they fully appreciate the contents of this chapter, or not.

Hopefully, this chapter has shed some light on the mysterious, and often misunderstood, subject of ballistics. On reflection, it's really pretty simple. Gravity causes bullets to drop towards the ground; how far they fall is determined by time in flight. Air resistance acts to slow a bullet's speed and limit how far it travels in a horizontal direction. A bullet's muzzle velocity and ballistic coefficient contribute to the down-range component of the bullet's flight. Gravity and air resistance working together give a bullet its trajectory.

The shooter's line of sight and the gun's bore are not one and the same. By making sight adjustments, bullet trajectory can be manipulated in relation to the shooter's line of sight in order to provide a useful aiming tool. By knowing the trajectory of hunting ammunition and using the concepts of point-blank range and mid-range trajectory, a gun can be zeroed to best meet the expected game and hunting conditions. Ballistic computer software is a valuable tool that can be used to guide decisions regarding cartridge selection and zero distances.

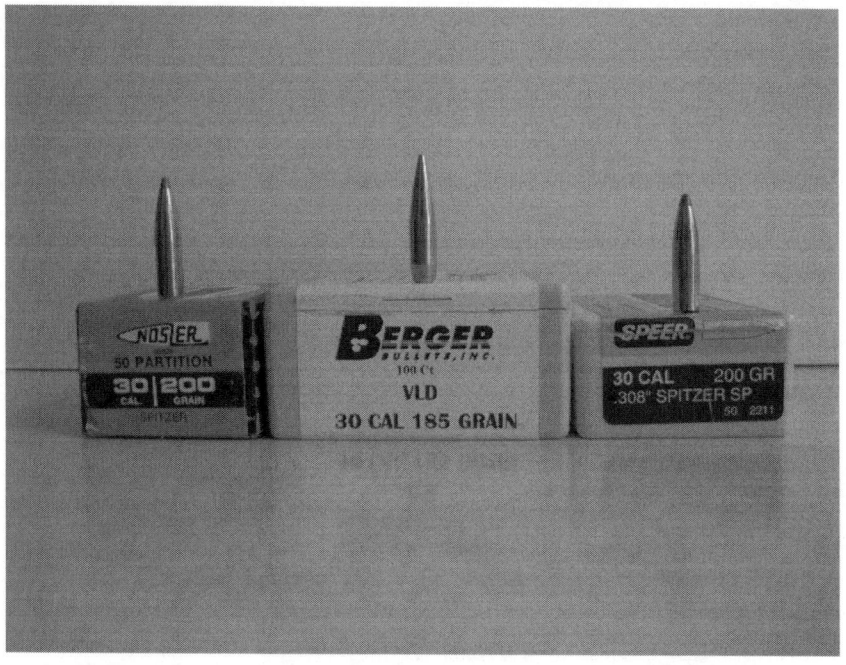

Three different .30 caliber bullets. The Nosler Partition has a ballistic coefficient of .481; the Berger VLD has a ballistic coefficient of .569; and the Speer has a ballistic coefficient of .556.

Sierra's Infinity Five ballistic software program. Ballistic software is an invaluable aid to shooters and hunters.

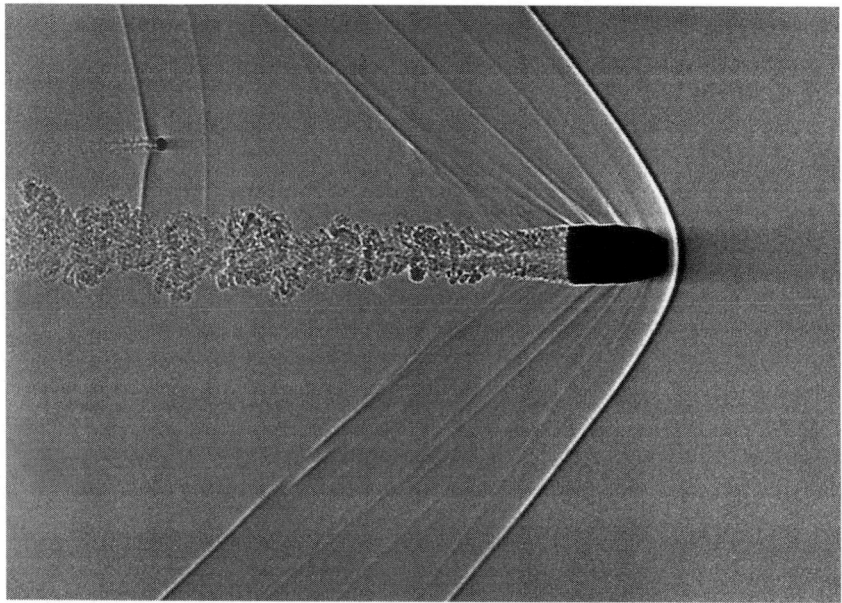

This is a shadowgraphic image of a supersonic bullet. Clearly visible are the v-shaped shockwaves made as the bullet plows through the atmosphere surrounding it. Also visible is the strong turbulence in the bullet's wake.
  Image from NASA, courtesy of Andrew Davidhazy/Rochester Institute of Technology

This is the re-creation of an actual shot I took at a Dall sheep in Alaska. The angle is 30 degrees. Shots along inclines are common in mountainous settings.
Photo by Steve Johnson

Shooting Up—Shooting Down

Let's go on a "pretend" hunt for mountain goats in British Columbia. You've been looking forward to this adventure for over a year and you expect it to be the toughest hunt of your life. Therefore, you've spent many hours preparing yourself physically and mentally. Since goats have a reputation as being a tough animal to kill, you don't want to find yourself "under-gunned" for the task. You also want the capability to reach out and "touch" a billy at long range. Although many potential cartridges would suffice for this hunt, you've selected a .300 Winchester magnum as your weapon of choice. Furthermore, you've decided to use the 200 grain Nosler® Partition™ bullet as your goat medicine.

For months prior to the hunt you have been practicing with this combination at ranges up to 400 yards. The load is sighted to hit 3″ high at 100 yards. From your research and range work you know the bullet has a muzzle velocity of approximately 2,800 feet per second (fps) and a ballistic coefficient of .481, and a trajectory that has it cross the line of sight (LOS) at 250 yards. The bullet hits 4″ low at 300 yards and 17″ low at 400 yards. That gives this round an effective point-blank range of 300 yards, assuming a tolerance of four inches above or below the LOS. Confident in your gun and your own abilities to hit goat-size targets out to 400 yards, you board the plane to Canada, full of anticipation.

On day five of your seven-day hunt, while you and

your guide are glassing the steep terrain surrounding you, he spots a lone goat on a rocky bench well below your position. After confirming that the goat is a good billy, your guide asks you if you can make the shot. Before answering, you carefully range the goat with your rangefinder, which reads 400 yards. That's at the limit of your ability, but it's a shot distance you've practiced repeatedly and feel you can make. Besides, it's late in the day and stalking closer, because of the topography, will take hours with the goat being out of sight the entire time. After considering all these factors, you decide to take the shot. Referring to your trajectory table, which you've taped to your gunstock, you confirm that the load prints 17" low at 400 yards. You use your backpack to supply a solid rest and raise your point of aim to compensate for the bullet's expected path at that distance, floating the cross hairs about six inches above the top of the goat's back. When everything seems steady you gently pull the trigger. At the shot the goat simply continues feeding, completely oblivious to the nearby danger.

As you chamber a fresh round your guide tells you he thinks the shot went high, but he's not sure. Desperate to make good on a second try, you recall reading an article that explained that shooting 400 yards at a steep angle is comparable to shooting 300 yards over level ground. Referring once again to your trajectory table, you note that the bullet should only hit 4" low at 300 yards. So you take aim again, raising the cross hairs this much higher than the junction of the lower and middle thirds of the goat's body. When you shoot this time your guide says he saw the bullet hit a rock just over the top of the goat's back.

At this point, the billy decides he has had enough and walks around a rock face and out of your life. To describe your state of mind as being dejected would be a gross understatement. In fact, you're absolutely sick. But what happened, and what could possibly explain such a horrible outcome in the face of two seemingly good trigger pulls? Before blaming the scope for magically failing to hold its zero, you might want to read on.

Our hypothetical hunter failed because he didn't understand the implications of shooting at uphill or downhill angles! But before I delve into an in-depth analysis of exactly what went wrong in the previous scenario, let me assure you that similar events happen countless times each and every hunting season. Shooting along paths that deviate from the horizontal is one of the most misunderstood topics in hunting, and with good reason. For years, gun writers and others have failed miserably at providing accurate and complete information, in an easily digestible format, to the hunting public. To be fair, this is not an easy subject to comprehend or explain, due to the mathematics and science that are central to this material. Nonetheless, it's certainly possible to convey to the interested reader what elements regarding shooting at angles they need be concerned with, and more importantly, what steps can be taken to ensure the accurate placement of bullets when shooting uphill and downhill. Before reading further, though, it's important to flush anything you think you know about this topic from your mind, and approach the material that follows as an unfilled vessel.

SIGHTING IN

In the previous chapter on ballistics I introduced several terms that are important to any discussion of bullet flight. Among those items are: bullet drop, line of sight (LOS), trajectory, "zero" range, muzzle velocity and ballistic coefficient. We'll make further use of these terms in this chapter. In order to discuss uphill and downhill shooting, we also need to introduce some new concepts and add to our vocabulary.

As you remember, we place sights on our guns and manipulate these sights in order to provide a tool that's useful for aiming across a spectrum of expected hunting situations. In doing so, we recognize the bullet initially leaves the barrel below the LOS, first crosses the LOS close to the shooter, travels above the LOS some distance before crossing the LOS a second time at the "zero" range, and thereafter travels below the LOS. Almost universally, when zeroing a gun this way, the shooting is done at or very near parallel to the earth's surface. Scientists use the term "inclined fire" to describe a situation where a firearm is initially sighted in this manner and the gun is later fired at a target which is located either uphill or downhill of the shooter, at some angle from the horizontal. The distance to the target for inclined-fire scenarios is referred to as the slant range.

In level-fire situations ballistic software can predict, or actual shooting can verify, where bullets will be relative to the LOS at any practical down-range distance. But those values apply only as long as the gun is maintained in a level posture. Once the muzzle is raised or lowered from the horizontal, the original shooting conditions have been altered. As a consequence, where a bullet passes in relation to the LOS at all ranges will have changed also. Stated differently, if a gun is zeroed at some known distance over level ground, it will no longer be zeroed at an equivalent slant range for inclined-fire situations.

Consider the following analogy: You want to determine how far your car will travel once you hit the brakes going sixty miles per hour. You conduct this test on a stretch of flat roadway and find it takes 100 feet for the car to come to a stop. Knowing that, would you assume the same vehicle would take 100 feet to stop on a significant incline? Of course not—you radically changed the conditions of the test! Common sense alone would predict a different result. Admittedly, for most of us, it's easier to comprehend that a car will take different distances to come to a stop on level ground and on an incline; it's more difficult to accept the fact that a bullet won't be in the same place it was during level fire, once the gun is elevated. But both are true.

Just as our car-stop experiment would yield one result on level ground and another when attempted on a hill, a bullet's trajectory when fired at 0° of elevation will be different than when fired at any positive or negative angle. Therefore, when shooting at an angle, it's a mistake to adjust your aim by simply applying bullet-LOS observations derived from level-fire conditions. For example, using our .300 Winchester round, we know the bullet hits 17″ below the LOS at 400 yards when fired over level ground. The same bullet will definitely not be 17″ below the LOS at a slant range of 400 yards when fired at 45°, or any other angle for that matter. So, raising the sights 17″ above the intended point of impact isn't justified (and may cause a miss) when shooting uphill or downhill. Before we can take proper aim when shooting at angles, we need more information.

BULLET PATHS

The first issue we need to consider is whether there's a difference between shooting at comparable uphill (elevation angle) and downhill (depression angle) lines of fire. Over the years, I've read all kinds of dissertations regarding this subject, many of them wrong. While it's true that bullet trajectories at depression angles are slightly flatter than their counterparts at equivalent elevation angles, the differences are insignificant across all inclines at practical hunting distances. Therefore, for our purposes, we can treat elevated fire and depressed fire as one and the same for any specified angle, as the trajectories are practically identical. That reality greatly simplifies what follows, as a separate analysis of numerically equivalent positive and negative angles is unnecessary.

The bullet-path height (or value) is the position of a bullet at a point along its trajectory, as measured from and perpendicular to the LOS. For a scoped rifle, the intersection of the cross hairs equates to the LOS. So, the bullet path at any point downrange is where that bullet will be in relation to where the cross hairs are located. Of course, the bullet can be above the LOS (positive value) or below the LOS (negative value). For inclined fire, it's important to note that the bullet-path height at all points along its course will be greater than the bullet-path height at the corresponding down-range points under level-fire conditions. This is true at all angles, but the steeper the shooting angle the greater the difference in bullet-path values at any point. In addition, as the slant range increases differences between level-fire and inclined-fire trajectories become more exaggerated. This phenomenon also occurs at all angles, but this departure is more pronounced at extreme shooting angles. In other words, there's much less room for error when shooting at steep angles and/or long distances.

Of course, there's a scientific explanation for why bullet-path values are greater for inclined fire than they are for level fire, but it's complicated. When shooting over level ground it's possible to make some observations. In fact, we can measure several key components of bullet flight, including bullet drop, time of flight and remaining velocity. If we catalog these items using our .300 Winchester round at a range of 400 yards, we discover that bullet drop is -43.25 inches, time of flight is .496 seconds and the remaining velocity is 2,089 feet per second. Bullet drop is normally expressed as a negative number because once a bullet leaves the gun's muzzle, it is always below this reference point. If we repeat this exercise, this time shooting at a 45° angle and a slant range of 400 yards, we'll discover virtually identical values for each of these measurements. In fact, we would find that these three parameters remained (nearly) constant no matter the angle of fire. This does make some sense, as the bullet does indeed travel a full 400 yards through the air, no matter what the firing angle is. And, it's reasonable to expect a bullet to take the same time to travel the same distance, and to lose the same amount of velocity along the way. So, what explains the differences in bullet path that I detailed earlier? The key lies in bullet drop, and how it is measured!

Bullet drop is always measured from the extended bore line to a point along the bullet's trajectory, but in a direction perpendicular to the earth's surface. At a uniform slant range, the only way bullet drop can remain constant (and it does) is if the bullet travels closer to the extended bore line as the incline becomes greater. By implication, this also means the bullet is located further from the LOS as the angle of fire becomes more severe (See Figure 1). Consequently, bullet-path values at all points along the bullet's trajectory increase as the barrel is raised (or lowered) from level fire to increasingly steeper angles.

If none of what I've said in the last two paragraphs makes sense or is interesting; that's okay, because you don't need this information to be able to shoot accurately on inclines. What you do need is fairly simple. Knowing the shooting angle and the slant range to the target are musts. They can be estimated by various means, but the newer "smart" rangefinders will give very accurate readings for both parameters with one push of a button. I strongly recommend their use, but caution is warranted. First, rangefinders don't always work. They rely on batteries, and some atmospheric conditions, such as snow and rain, can interfere with accurate readings. So you should have some fall-back means of estimating both distance and angle. Second, you must be careful about the information the rangefinder feeds you. Although the "smart" technology will provide a "ballistic" range to target; depending on the manufacturer, this may only equate to the effective horizontal shooting distance. As I will show later, aiming using this approach may still result in poorly placed shots. My advice is to use the rangefinder whenever possible, but only to obtain the slant range (LOS) to target and the angle of fire. As you'll see, we'll use alter-

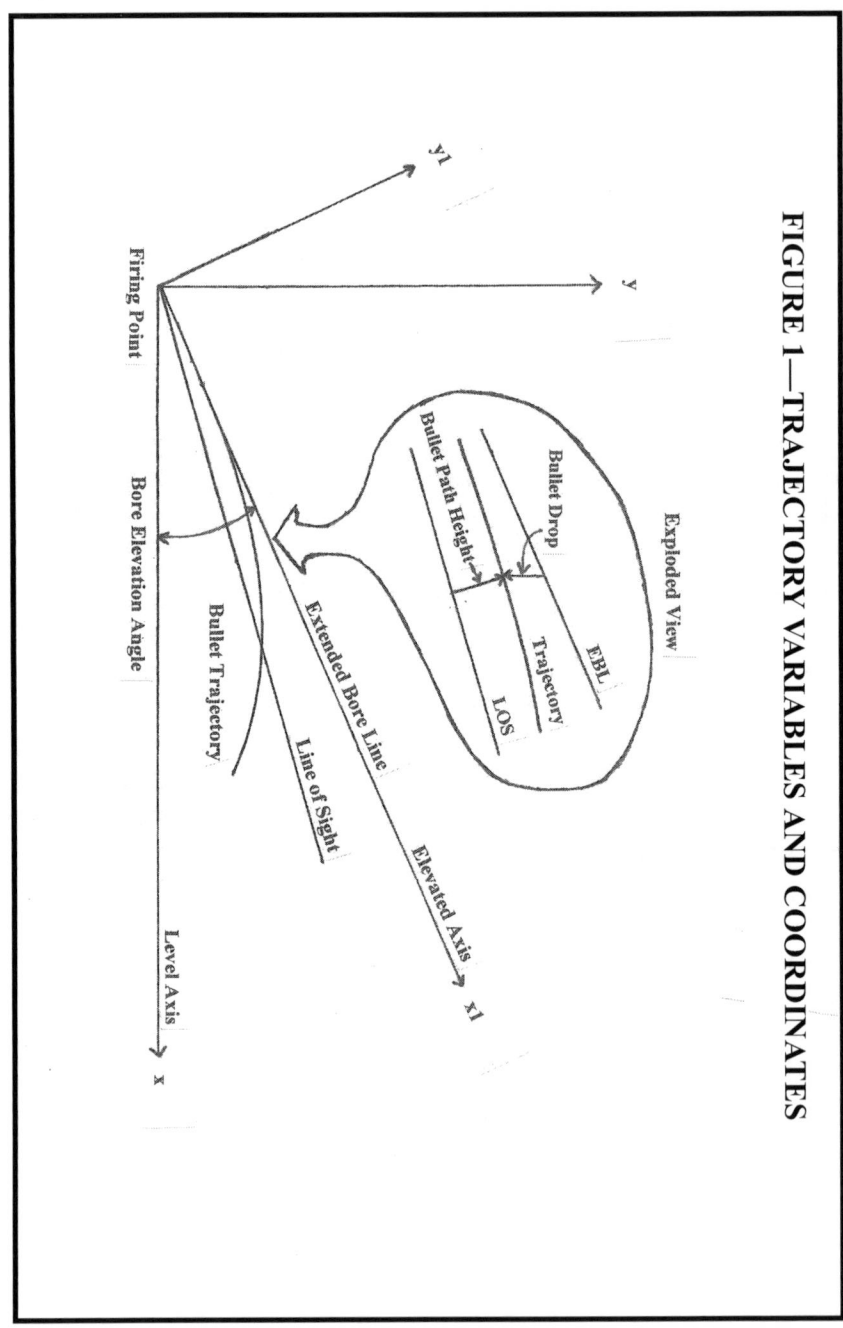

FIGURE 1—TRAJECTORY VARIABLES AND COORDINATES

nate means to turn those values into an accurate firing solution.

The key to determining the correct aiming point in inclined fire situations is: knowing where the bullet will be relative to the LOS at the slant-range distance to the target. We must start with the only yardstick at hand—the bullet-path values derived from a level-fire condition. Fortunately, ballistic software programs, which I mentioned in the last chapter, are just the ticket for developing the needed information. All we have to do is ask the program the right questions.

If we plug in the relevant data (muzzle velocity, ballistic coefficient and sight height) for the .300 Winchester ammunition we've been using, my Sierra® Infinity program calculates bullet-path values as seen in Table 1 (0° firing angle), when shooting over level ground. I've arbitrarily limited the maximum range to 500 yards, for simplicity. Remember, positive values mean the bullet is above the LOS at a specified range, whereas negative values describe a situation where the bullet is below the LOS. Once the program has this level-fire baseline calculated, you can ask it to compute bullet-path values for inclined-fire situations by specifying an angle. I have included these subsequent computations for angles of 30°, 45° and 60° in Table 1.

If we study this table for a moment, we can make some important observations. First, at all angles the bullet-path value is -1.50˝ at the muzzle, reflecting the fact that the sights are mounted this same distance above the bore's centerline. Next, you can clearly see that the gun is zeroed at 250 yards, because the bullet-path value is zero at this distance when the shooting angle is 0°. Reading the table from left to right at each range, you'll notice that as the angle of fire becomes progressively steeper, the bullet-path values get larger. This not only supports the observation that inclined fire results in a higher bullet trajectory than level fire, but that the magnitude

TABLE 1—COMPARATIVE BULLET-PATH VALUES (inches)

Angle of Fire

Range (yards)	0°	30°	45°	60°
0	-1.50	-1.50	-1.50	-1.50
50	1.36	1.43	1.52	1.64
100	3.03	3.34	3.71	4.19
150	3.42	4.13	4.98	6.09
200	2.45	3.74	5.29	7.31
250	0.00	2.07	4.55	7.79
300	-4.03	-0.97	2.69	7.48
350	-9.77	-5.50	-0.39	6.30
400	-17.36	-11.64	-4.77	4.20
450	-26.93	-19.50	-10.58	1.09
500	-38.67	-29.24	-17.92	-3.10

.300 Winchester, 200 grain Nosler Partition bullet (B.C.=.481) @ 2,800 fps

of this higher trajectory is dependent on the shooting angle. Thus, steep shooting angles result in relatively higher trajectories than do shallow shooting angles.

Now that we've generated the information in Table 1, how is it used to provide the correct aiming point when shooting at some angle? To begin, let's contemplate what happens at a range of 250 yards. As I just mentioned, when the shooting angle is 0° the gun is zeroed at this distance, and Table 1 reflects this fact. But notice what happens when we start shooting at angles. Clearly, the gun is no longer zeroed at 250 yards during any inclined-fire scenario. Table 1 tells us that at a slant range of 250 yards the bullet is 2.07″ above the LOS at a 30° angle, 4.55″ above the LOS at a 45° angle and 7.79″ above the LOS at a 60° angle. Stated another way, a bullet will hit 2.07″ above the cross hairs when shooting at a 30° angle and a slant range of 250 yards, and so on. If we want the bullet to hit the proper spot, Table 1 dictates that we lower our aim by a corresponding amount at each angle. Thus, if we were shooting at an animal at a slant range of 250 yards along 60° incline, we should aim about 8″ below where we'd like the bullet to strike.

By referencing Table 1, similar aiming corrections can be derived for other potential shots of varying length and angle. Keep in mind that sight corrections needn't always be in a downward direction. For example, if we evaluate a slant range of 350 yards and a 30° shooting angle, we notice the bullet path is 5.50″ below the LOS. Therefore, we would need to elevate our aim by this amount in order to place the bullet accurately. If the same shot were taken over level ground the bullet path would be 9.77″ below the LOS, necessitating an upward aiming adjustment of almost 10 inches. So, while it's true that shooting on inclines always requires us to aim lower than we would for a shot of similar length on flat terrain, that doesn't mean we always aim low in absolute terms!

At this juncture, now that we're all better informed

about shooting at angles, let's revisit the hypothetical goat hunt at the beginning of the chapter and try and figure out why our hunter's first shot missed. As you recall, I didn't specify an exact shooting angle, although I mentioned the terrain was steep and that the goat was well below the hunter. We have come to realize that uphill and downhill shooting can be treated identically, so the fact that the target is below the hunter isn't significant. Just for kicks, let's assume the angle is 60° and analyze what happened. From Table 1, a bullet will be 4.20″ above the LOS when fired at a 60° angle at a target 400 yards away. That suggests lowering aim by about 4″ to arrive at the correct sight picture. Our hunter, unfortunately, chose to employ level-fire data for an inclined-fire shooting problem. Although it was inappropriately applied, the level-fire information at our shooter's disposal predicted the bullet to be 17.36″ below the LOS at 400 yards. Consequently, he raised his aim by this amount, adding this entire error to the 4″ of error he accumulated by not lowering the sights in the first place. As a result, he missed his intended point of aim, high, by over 21 inches! No wonder the goat seemed unperturbed. Not many hunters are going home with game—and happy memories—if their aim is off by twenty-one inches. I believe most errant shots at game are high misses, most of which are caused by a similar lack of understanding regarding inclined fire.

 We know we need the angle of fire and the slant range to be able to shoot accurately in inclined-fire situations. With those inputs in hand, ballistic software will give us the corresponding bullet-path values, which can then be used to correct aim. Since it's normally not practical to bring our computers hunting with us, how can we best access the data we need to aim properly in the field? Simple—the computer can be used at home to crank out the bullet-path values for various angles and target distances, and then a "cheat sheet" can be created from the data. This sheet can be carried while hunting and referenced prior to shooting. Then, once you're in position for a shot, all you need to do is measure or estimate the distance to target and the angle of fire, and read the correct hold from the sheet. For those distances and angles that fall between the established values, it's a fairly simple matter to interpolate the best aiming solution.

A representative "cheat sheet" for our .300 Winchester round is shown in Figure 2. I rounded the bullet-path values to the nearest inch in order to give the sheet a less cluttered look, and I included information regarding wind drift. I also added notes which instruct the user to "aim low by" for positive values and "aim high by" for negative values. The last thing anyone needs in a stressful hunting situation is mental fog, casting doubts as to whether the proper course of action is to raise or lower aim. Explicit instructions help avoid confusion. The handiest place for this shooting aid is taped to the gunstock, where it is always immediately available. Clear packing tape covering the entire sheet protects it from the elements. It would also be wise to carry a duplicate laminated sheet elsewhere, just in case.

Earlier I mentioned that it's wise to have some backup method of estimating range and shooting angle, in case the rangefinder isn't working. Armed with a better understanding of inclined fire and your cheat sheet, rational decisions can still be made regarding the proper sight picture, even when the exact distance and shooting angle aren't known. Personally, I believe it's generally easier to estimate angle than it is to discern range. Nevertheless, the cheat sheet will detail the implications of misjudging either parameter.

As an example, let's say you're confident the shooting angle is close to 30°, but you can only approximate range somewhere between 300 and 400 yards. Referring to Figure 2, you understand that you need to aim 1″ high for a shot of 300 yards, 6″ high if shooting 350 yards and 12″ high for 400 yards.

Assuming your range estimation is good enough that the target is actually somewhere in this hundred-yard interval, there's an 11″ worst-case exposure in aiming error. That is: if you aim as though the animal is 300 yards distant and it's really 400 yards away (or vice versa), your aim will be off by 11 inches. Given this fact, it may be prudent to "split the difference" and aim as though the quarry is 350 yards away, even though you don't know the actual yardage. That way, you limit your potential aiming error to only 5″ if the range turns out to be 300 yards and 6″ if the target is 400 yards away. Obviously, for target distances inside these extremes aiming error would be even less.

FIGURE 2—CHEAT SHEET .300 WINCHESTER

	0°	30°	45°	60°
50	1	1	2	2
100	3	3	4	4
150	3	4	5	6
200	2	4	5	7
250	0	2	5	8
300	-4	-1	3	7
350	-10	-6	0	6
400	-17	-12	-5	4
450	-27	-20	-11	1
500	-39	-29	-18	-3

+ AIM LOW BY
- AIM HIGH BY
10-mph crosswind
3″@200
6″@300
12″@400

The advantage to this approach is that you're hedging your bets, and giving yourself a reasonable chance to make a killing shot, even though you don't have all the information you would like. Just be aware, however, if your range estimation is so poor that the animal isn't even located in the yardage interval you're contemplating, you will likely miss. The important point is that with accurate bullet-path data at your disposal, you can make informed decisions regarding aim, even when the rangefinder is on the fritz.

OTHER METHODS OF DETERMINING AIM

In the previous section I spent a great deal of time explaining what happens with bullet trajectories during inclined fire and why. I also presented what I believe to be the most practical way of dealing with inclined-fire scenarios while hunting. In my opinion, using ballistic software to calculate relevant aiming information is the gold standard for this kind of work. And, carrying this information in the field for reference is the easiest and most dependable way for a hunter to make the correct aiming adjustments in most hunting situations.

The reader should know, however, that there are other methods that can be used to assist aim in inclined-fire situations. The limitations of these methods should be known also. At their root, these approaches all involve a fairly simple mathematical model that uses level-fire data, combined with the shooting angle and slant range, to predict the bullet path for a particular shot. The mathematical models vary, as does the effectiveness of each in providing good aiming approximations.

The oldest and most commonly applied of these approaches is sometimes referred to as the "Rifleman's Rule." The basic premise is that inclined fire can be treated as though one were only shooting over the horizontal component of the slant-range distance to target. The assumption is that gravity is acting on the bullet as if it were fired this distance over level ground. Thus, this horizontal component is sometimes referred to as the "corrected-for-gravity" distance to target.

Basic geometry tells us that for a right triangle, the hypotenuse (slant range) is longer than either of the triangle's legs. If we know the angle of fire and the slant range, the trigonometric cosine of the angle can be used to calculate the horizontal leg of the triangle (See Figure 3). The shooter then treats this as the actual target distance and aims based on level-fire predictions of bullet path. Previously, I cautioned readers about rangefinders that might use this approach to provide a "ballistic" range to target. I also referenced this method for our goat hunter's second shot.

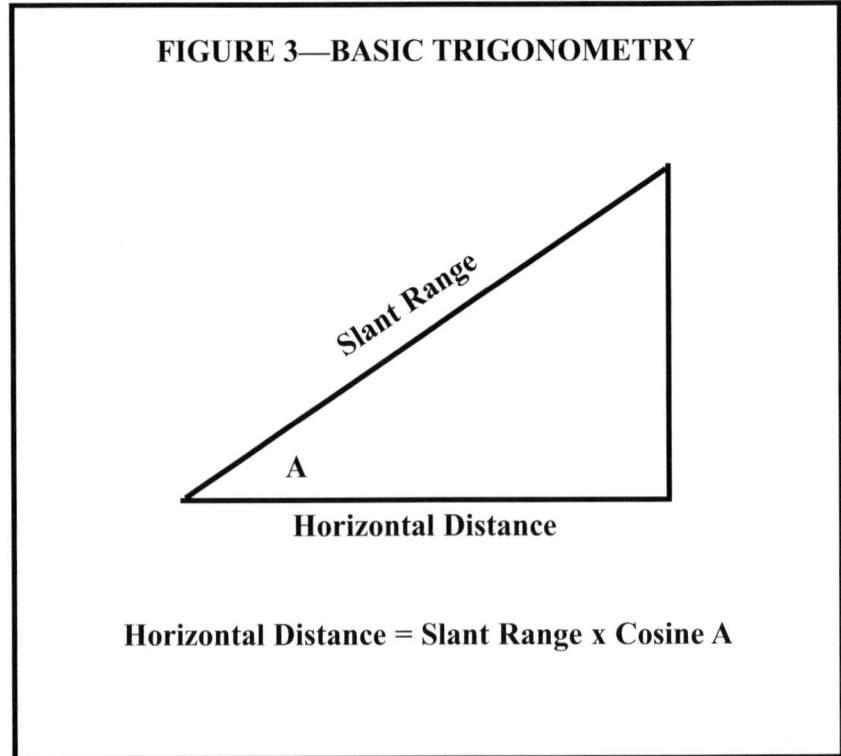

If we return once again to that goat hunt, we can examine the effectiveness of the Rifleman's Rule (RR). When combined with a slant range of 400 yards and a depression angle of fire of 60°, the effective horizontal distance to target can be calculated to be 200 yards (400 x Cosine 60° = 400 x .5 = 200). Using level-fire data, the bullet path is 2.45˝ above the LOS at 200 yards (Refer to Table 1, 200 yards at 0°). If applying the RR, the shooter would aim that much low. In actuality, the bullet will be 4.20˝ above the LOS for this shot (Table 1, 400 yards at 60°). Therefore, the correct hold for this situation would entail lowering aim by 4 inches. Obviously, at least for this example, the RR only partially accounted for the necessary aiming correction. In all likelihood, our hunter would have still killed the goat if this rule had been correctly followed. Of course, our shooter misapplied the rule, as he didn't know the angle or the bullet-path value, and arbitrarily used 300 yards as the horizontal distance to target. As you remember, he raised his aim by 4 inches (Table 1, 300 yards at 0°), resulting in a total aiming error of 8˝ and a second missed opportunity.

Obviously, the Rifleman's Rule doesn't work perfectly. If you took time to make similar comparisons of the aiming adjustments predicted by this rule and the ballistic software gold standard, you would find it loses its effectiveness at ranges approaching 400 yards, especially at steep angles. However, at shorter ranges and shallow angles the RR gives a good approximation in correcting aim. For example, let's see what adjustment in aim this rule would forecast for a shooting situation in which the angle is 30° and the slant range is 300 yards. By doing the math (300 x Cosine 30° = 300 x .866 = 260), we determine the horizontal distance to the target to be about 260 yards. Using the level-fire bullet-path value closest to this distance (250 yards), the RR tells us to hold dead on. On the other hand, the highly accurate software program advises us to aim high by 1 inch (Table 1, 300 yards at 30°). A one-inch discrepancy is insignificant, and would most certainly result in a clean kill.

I'm aware of two additional methods that can be used to estimate where to aim in inclined-fire scenarios. The first of these methods has been called the "Improved Rifleman's Rule" in a paper by Mike Brown, and calculates the needed aiming adjustment by: measuring the inclination angle; measuring the slant range to target; referencing the bullet-path value from the level trajectory at a horizontal distance equal to the slant range; multiplying this bullet-path value by the cosine of the inclination angle to obtain an adjusted bullet-path value; and using this adjusted bullet-path value to correct aim.[1] As applied to our goat hunter, this approach predicts a bullet path 8.68″ below the LOS (-17.36 x Cosine 60° = -17.36 x .5 = -8.68). Therefore, aim should be elevated by about 9 inches. This would result in the shot being 13″ high because the correct hold is 4″ low! That's 8″ better than if pure level-fire data had been used, but still not good enough to kill the goat. As you can see, at least in this instance, the application of the Improved Rifleman's Rule (IRR) would result in significantly more aiming error than if the original RR (2″ aiming error) were used. So you may rightly ask, where's the improvement?

Extensive analysis of these two methods would allow some generalizations to be made. Application of the RR would produce decent corrections at moderate ranges across most practical shooting angles, whereas the IRR exhibits strength at much longer ranges, but only at shallow angles. Neither approach shines at angles greater than 30° and ranges approaching 400 yards.

The final method of adjusting aim during inclined fire is called Sierra's Approach, because it was discovered by ballistician William T. McDonald while working for the compa-

[1] "Inclined Fire," William T. McDonald, www.exteriorballistics.com, June 2003

ny in the 1980s. This method involves: measuring the inclination angle; measuring the slant range; referencing both the bullet drop and bullet path from the level trajectory at a distance equivalent to the slant range; changing the algebraic sign of the bullet drop number to be positive, then multiplying this number by the quantity [1.0 − Cosine inclination angle]; adding this result to the bullet-path value (level trajectory) to obtain an adjusted bullet path; and using this adjusted bullet-path value to correct aim.[2]

Let's work the math for our goat-hunting scenario and see just how favorably this approach compares to the aiming correction dictated by the ballistic software and the previous two methods. The only additional information we need is the bullet drop at 400 yards, which is -43.25 inches. As you may remember, I stated earlier that bullet drop remains almost constant at like target distances, no matter the angle of fire. After changing the drop to a positive number, we first multiply this quantity by [1.0 − Cosine 60°]. The result is 21.67 inches (43.25 × [1.0 - .5] = 43.25 × .5 = 21.67). Next, this value is added to the bullet-path value at a level-fire distance of 400 yards, resulting in an adjusted bullet path of 4.31 inches (21.67 - 17.36 = 4.31). As you recall, the Infinity software gives the bullet path for the same shooting situation as 4.20 inches. Both methods dictate that aim be lowered by 4 inches. By comparison, the RR under-corrected aim by approximately 2″ and the IRR over-corrected aim by 13″ for the same shooting problem.

Plainly, the Sierra Method developed by Mr. McDonald proved extremely accurate for this set of circumstances. If you were to perform an extensive analysis of the Sierra Method, you would find that it produces highly accurate aiming approximations across all practical shooting angles and hunting ranges. This capability makes it a very valuable

---

[2] "Inclined Fire," William T. McDonald, www.exteriorballistics.com, June 2003

tool for determining proper aiming solutions for inclined-fire situations.

The beauty of having a simple formula, which reasonably predicts bullet paths, is that a computer isn't necessary to provide aiming corrections for inclined-fire situations. Instead, a hand-held portable calculator, one which can perform algebraic and trigonometric functions, can be used in the field to supply the necessary hold. Let me elaborate.

Once in shooting position, the hunter determines the distance to target, most commonly with the rangefinder. In addition, the shooting angle is ascertained. This value can also be derived using a rangefinder possessing "smart" technology. Alternatively, angle can be determined by means of an angle degree indicator which attaches directly to the firearm. This tool consists of a weighted wheel enclosed by an external housing. The wheel is free to move and maintains a constant orientation relative to the earth, and the housing is calibrated to display the shooting angle as the gun is tipped along an incline. The angle cosine indicator is a similar tool, but it is calibrated to indicate the relevant cosine value for whatever angle the gun assumes. Since all the aforementioned means of approximating aim (RR, IRR and Sierra's Method) rely on the cosine of the inclination angle, the angle cosine indicator eliminates the need to convert the raw angle to its cosine equivalent.

The advantage of using this approach is that sight corrections are always made based upon the exact target distance and shooting angle. Therefore, the interpolations that are sometimes necessary when using a cheat sheet can be avoided. Keep in mind, however, this method necessitates taking extra gear into the field, and it still requires the hunter to have relevant ballistic data (or a means to calculate it) on their person. For instance, even when using the simplest of formulas (i.e., Rifleman's Rule), at least one mathematical calculation must be performed and the shooter would still need to reference the level-fire bullet path for the adjusted target distance prior to shooting. Obviously, more complex aiming formulas require more information, more manipulations and more time to arrive at a firing solution. Even so, for some hunters, this system may be preferable to my favored means of correcting aim—a cheat sheet containing bullet-path data at fifty-yard intervals.

I should also mention that hand-held, portable computers cabable of performing ballistic computations are available. They are, however, expensive. In addition, they rely on batteries, expertise and time to provide shooting solutions. On balance, I sincerely believe most hunters are better served by the simplicity afforded them by a cheat sheet.

If inclined-fire situations can be expected during the course of hunting (and rare are the occasions when they won't be) it's important to understand what's occurring regarding bullet flight, and have a means of making the appropriate adjustments in aim.

Hopefully, by now it's evident to all that we can't simply treat uphill or downhill shooting situations as though they were equivalent to shooting the same distance over level ground. Shooting on inclines isn't difficult; it simply requires a change in mindset—and more information—when compared to shooting over level ground. If given the shooting angle and the slant-range distance to the target, ballistic software can predict where the bullet will be in relation to the LOS for any shooting problem. Once this bullet-path value is known, the appropriate adjustment to aim can be made to ensure the bullet hits its intended mark.

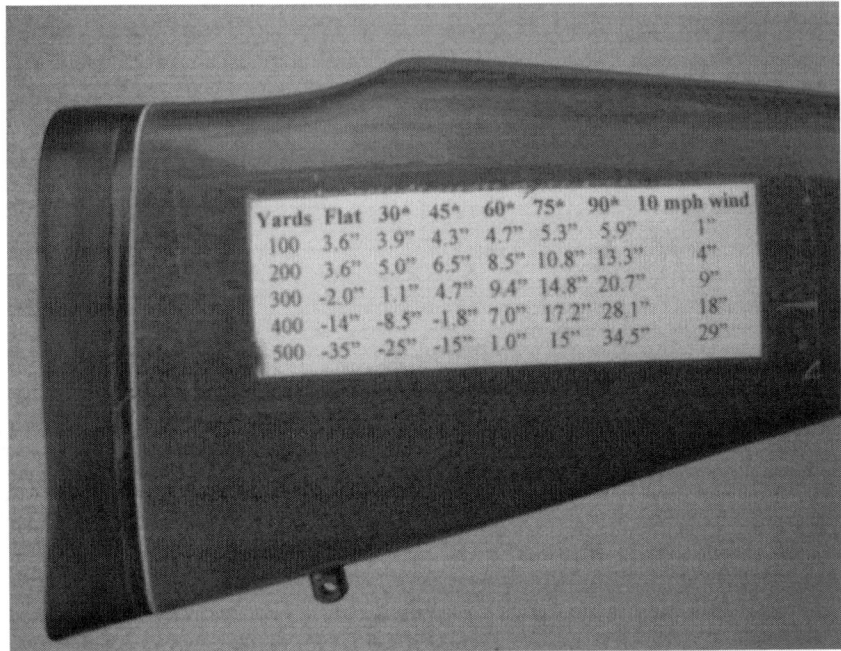

An example of a "cheat" sheet taped to the gunstock, where information needed to determine proper aim can be readily accessed before shooting.

This is the result of a real hunt for mountain goats, one where the outcome turned out much better than the hypothetical hunter described in this chapter.
Photo by Roy Milner

The process of shooting a gun isn't as complicated and doesn't have as many moving parts as does this clock-tower mechanism, but good shooting form is vital to the big-game hunter.

Good Shooting Mechanics

Most people wouldn't know it, but there are mechanical aspects involved in shooting a gun. They may be less obvious than, say, those inherent to a golf swing, but they do exist and their proper execution is just as important to hunting success as a flawless swing is to scoring well on the golf course. If we break down shooting into its basic elements, the classic fundamental concepts of proper shooting form are: sight alignment, sight picture, trigger pull and follow-through. Superimposed over these building blocks is breath control.

Sight alignment is the relationship between the front and rear sights of a firearm. It is a term that is most applicable to guns with iron or open sights, be it handgun, rifle or shotgun. Whatever the particular style or configuration of such aiming implements—and there are many—it is crucial that the two sights be correctly positioned in relation to each other, if the shot is to fly true. These days, the vast majority of big-game hunters are availing themselves of telescopic sights to aim their rifles. Since scopes contain a single aiming device in a single plane, there is no need to align one sight with the other. Indeed, this feature constitutes one of the advantages of using a modern scope, especially for those of us over forty years old. The lenses in older eyes lack the youthful flexibility required to focus on up-close objects. This condition makes it difficult to effectively use iron-sighting systems. Whether one chooses a scope for reason of eyesight or because of some other advantage it offers, the net result is one less step to consider, one less skill to acquire and one less place where error can be introduced into the process of shooting.

Sight picture is the proper relationship of the target to the sight(s). For guns sporting open sights, the sights must first be aligned before the target is positioned relative to the front sight. For scoped guns, the cross hairs (or other internal reticle) are held to ensure the bullet strikes the target. In the special case of big-game hunting, that means the desired location for bullet placement is within the animal's vital organs. Therefore, for the most routine of shots, the proper sight picture would show the cross hairs superimposed over the center of this area. However, in less ordinary circumstances, such as shooting at extreme range and into stiff crosswinds, the proper sight picture may show the cross hairs located completely off the animal, in order to account for the expected bullet drop and wind deflection.

Of course, knowing where the sights should be held for any particular situation and keeping them there are two entirely different things. Unless a firearm is locked into a vise, there is some unavoidable wandering of the sights about the target. This is sometimes referred to as the "arc of movement," and it becomes more exaggerated as the shooting position grows less stable. Consequently, assuming the range to target is equivalent, someone shooting off-hand can expect to experience more "sight wobble" than they will shooting from a steadier position, such as sitting. This factor explains why, generally speaking, the effective range of off-hand shots is appreciably less than those taken sitting, regardless of who's doing the shooting. In addition, sight movement can be expected to become a more significant problem as range increases, no matter the position used for shooting. Among marksmen of differing abilities, the most skilled and successful shots are those who are best able to minimize the arc of sight movement, and those who can break the shot at exactly the right moment during this movement—which brings us to the subject of trigger pull.

A smooth trigger pull—sometimes called a trigger "squeeze"—is essential to the accurate placement of shots. The goal, of course, is for the gun to discharge while the sights hover over the intended point of aim. This sounds like a fairly simple proposition, but much goes into its actual accomplishment.

Over the years, I've read numerous books and articles which have discussed the proper approach to freeing a gun's firing pin. Two different schools of thought have seemingly emerged. One camp feels the best results are obtained when the gun discharges by "surprise." In other words, the person doing the shooting becomes so intensely focused on the act of executing the shot, there's no anticipation as to exactly when the gun will go off. The other group believes the trigger must be finely controlled during the pull, in order to ensure the gun is pointing in the correct place when it fires. To do otherwise risks having the gun discharge when the sights aren't aimed at the vitals.

In my view, it really matters little which camp best describes any individual's approach to trigger control. What's more important is: how well the shot is ultimately executed, and how successful each hunter is at taking game cleanly. Stated differently, the end result is more important than the means used to get there. But despite my previous statement, I have definite thoughts regarding the best way to develop good trigger skills and how to become the best, most versatile shot on big game.

For those shots taken under very steady circumstances, where the sights move only slightly and never waver outside the vital zone, either of the aforementioned approaches to trigger control will work. In fact, in these situations you can blow an otherwise easy shot by being too careful and taking too long to pull the trigger. The animal could move or you could lose your concentration. If the sight picture is so steady that the sights never leave the vitals, all one must do is be smooth and not yank the sights off target while pulling the trigger.

Now, consider a different circumstance, one where the sights wobble so much that they're not always within an animal's kill zone. If one belongs to the gun-going-off-by-surprise school, there's a decent chance the rifle will discharge when the sights aren't on the vitals. Surprise, you missed! However, if one is able to adequately control the trigger, it's possible to break the shot when the sight picture is perfect (or nearly so), resulting in a clean kill. This is not an easy skill to acquire, however. The greater the amount of sight wobble, the more expertise is required to make the shot. Because so many big-game hunting situations produce shot opportunities that aren't as solid as one would like, I strongly believe hunters will attain substantial benefit by developing this kind of trigger control, to whatever extent is ultimately possible. Some will progress further and more rapidly than others, but everyone can profit by learning how to make the gun fire on demand.

The first requirement in developing such talent is a responsive trigger. Trying to precisely manipulate some stubborn and stiff trigger with excessive travel is nearly impossible. So what characteristics define the desirable hunting trigger? The force required to disengage the trigger should be about three pounds. If the trigger pull is much lighter than that, the risk of unintentionally discharging the weapon goes up, especially with gloved hands. If the pull is much heavier than three pounds, fine control is jeopardized. The trigger should also disengage crisply (little creep) and its overall travel should be minimal. Unfortunately, even though many factory rifles have otherwise good triggers, their pulls are often set quite heavy due to reasons of potential product liability. If you own such a gun, someone must make the appropriate adjustments to obtain the desired three-pound pull. If you aren't knowledgeable enough to do this without compromising safety, have a reputable gunsmith do it for you. The quality and adjustability of a gun's trigger is a primary consideration for me when purchasing a new firearm.

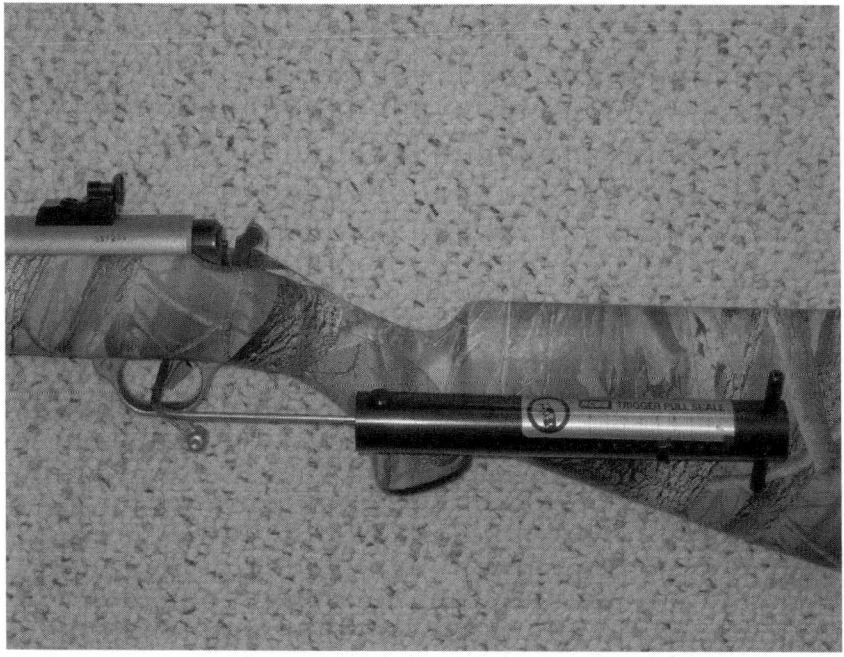

This photo shows a trigger-pull gauge, which reads just over three pounds of pull. It's impossible to develop good shooting form with a poor trigger.

Once a hunting rifle is fitted with a suitable trigger, the second pillar of trigger skill is the education of the index finger to the intricacies of that particular trigger. And like almost all learning, that doesn't come automatically. Only by repeated experience over time can the finger "know" exactly how much remaining pressure is required to free the firing pin. Fortunately, this kind of intimate feel can be substantially developed from the comfort of one's living room and without the use of live rounds. Known as "dry firing," pulling the trigger on an empty chamber, dummy round or so-called "snap" cap, is an excellent and cheap way to further one's shooting ability. When practicing in this manner, treat every pull of the trigger as if a shot is being taken at an animal. It's important the gun be shouldered and the hands and trigger finger placed exactly as they would if hunting. In addition, concentration on shot execution and follow-through should be maintained. Otherwise, there is a risk of incorporating bad habits into one's shooting form. You really can't do too much dry firing, and you needn't worry about harming your gun's firing pin in the process. However, before contemplating such exercises, it's absolutely essential for reasons of safety, to visually verify that the gun (magazine and chamber) is unloaded!

I believe it makes some difference as to which part of the finger is used to contact the trigger. The ideal place is the center of the pad before the first joint of the index finger. That's because this area is flat, sensitive, offers the most control and best allows for a straight rearward pull without applying lateral torque to the gun. Some small variation of trigger contact about this pad can be expected, due to differences in hand size and shooter preference. However, the crease of the first joint should be avoided when executing the trigger pull, because it offers neither sensitivity nor control.

The goal of the trigger pull is to move the trigger directly rearward until it releases, so that the sights aren't disturbed in the process. Besides the trigger finger, the rest of the shooting hand has some bearing on whether the sight picture is disrupted during the pull. There's a normal tendency for the thumb and non-trigger fingers to tightly grasp a rifle about the gun's tang when shooting, especially in stressful situations. "Choking" the tang in this way should be consciously avoided because it introduces extraneous forces into the act of pulling the trigger. A simple way to prevent these unhelpful shooting stresses is to alter the thumb's position. Rather than allowing the thumb to cross over the tang, it is preferable to place this digit parallel to the long axis of the gun, pointing towards the muzzle. This serves to relax the entire hand, leaving the trigger finger to do its job unaffected by the remainder of the hand.

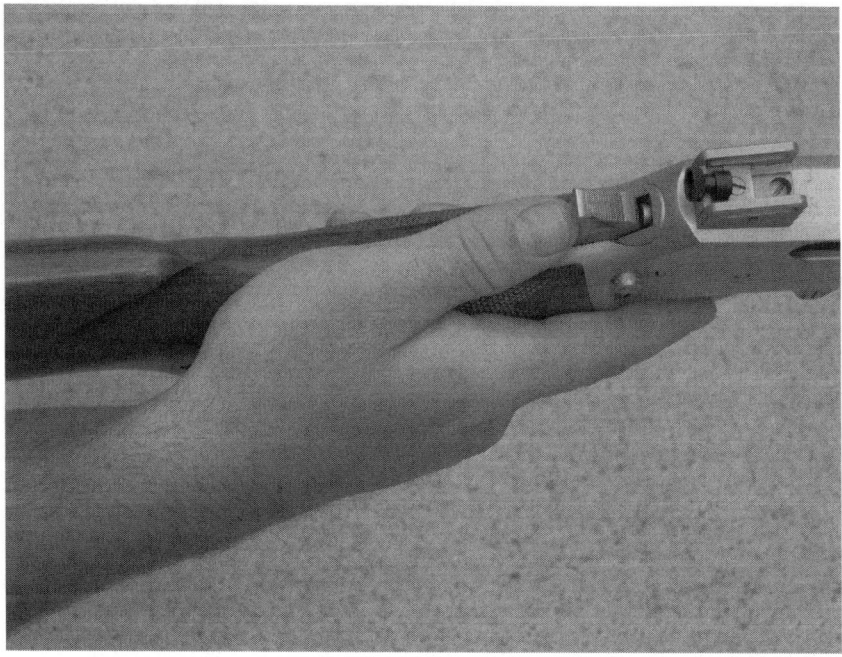

This shows the proper position of the thumb of the shooting hand. This posture results in a more relaxed hand and less stress on the trigger pull than when the thumb grips the rifle across the tang.

Besides a responsive trigger and intimate familiarity with that trigger, the final ingredient in getting the gun to fire on demand is actual shooting under less-than-steady conditions. One can't learn to deal with wobbly sights by shooting from a bench rest. So, practice from off-hand, but start at relatively short range where sight movement will be less noticeable. Since ammunition is cheap and recoil light, the best gun to use for this purpose is the venerable .22 caliber rifle. What you'll soon discover is that although the sights wander, they do so with some predictability. The trick is to recognize when the sights are about to swing back to the desired sight picture, and finish the trigger pull as they do so. The trigger cannot be yanked, however, or the shot will miss its mark. Acquiring this skill takes lots of practice. Once proficiency is achieved at short range, the difficulty of the exercise can be increased by extending the distance to target. At some range, however, expect sight wobble to be so great that shooting accuracy diminishes below the level which would be considered ethically acceptable on game. So, shots at animals should be limited to those distances where true expertise has been demonstrated.

Although I suggested the off-hand position as the easiest way to intentionally introduce sight instability into practice routines, the same concept is applicable to other shooting positions, as well. Once sight wobble can be managed from one shooting position, the same amount of sight movement can expect to be mastered when shooting from other postures. The difference is: as the shooting position becomes steadier, equivalent degrees of sight wobble will occur at increasingly greater target distances. In other words, one may not experience the same amount of sight movement found while shooting off-hand at 100 yards, until taking aim at 300 yards from prone. In any event, maximum shooting distance should be considered situational. One's expertise in dealing with a given amount of sight instability, as it's experienced from the most stable shooting position available at the time, will ultimately determine the exact yardage.

In the language of shooting, follow-through refers to maintaining the correct sight picture until after the bullet has exited the barrel. If the sights are disturbed prior to the bullet leaving the gun, the shot will likely miss its mark. There are two distinct intervals that contribute to the total span of time encompassing the follow-through period. The first interval comprises the elapsed time from when the trigger breaks to when the firing pin strikes the primer. This is referred to as lock time, and it is a mechanical feature specific to the firearm one is using. Some guns have faster lock times than do others. Obviously, all other things being equal, guns with faster lock times would be preferred over those that are mechanically slower. The second interval starts when the primer ignites and ends when the bullet exits the barrel. The cartridge and its specific components—primer, powder and bullet—determine how long this interval lasts. In total, the concept of follow-through is relevant for mere fractions of a second in modern center-fire rifles. In more primitive weapons, such as those of flintlock design, the period of time between trigger release and bullet exit is significantly longer, and follow-through becomes much more important to good marksmanship.

Correct breathing can help one shoot well, while incorrect breathing can adversely affect performance. It stands to reason that no one can be truly steady while inhaling or exhaling, no matter how stable the shooting posture might otherwise be. Therefore, to realize maximum stability, the shot must be broken during a pause between breaths. The most common recommendation is for the shooter to take a full breath and then release approximately half of the lungs' volume, just before completing the trigger pull. Doing so limits body movement while leaving sufficient air in the lungs to prevent oxygen-starved tissues—at least for a short while.

If the shot cannot be completed before it becomes necessary to replenish depleted oxygen stores, it's best to start the sequence anew. Too often, as we struggle to steady the sights, hunters try to stay with a shot for too long. The result is an increasingly quivering stance, a sense of immediacy and desperation, and a poor outcome. Never be afraid to back away from a deteriorating situation, whether due to diminished oxygen or some other cause, and regroup. It only takes a few seconds to collect oneself, take a couple of deep breaths and start the process over. Quite often, a second go-around will seem steadier than the first, and there'll be plenty of air on hand to successfully complete the shot.

Besides the previously discussed shooting fundamentals, there are several additional factors that can contribute to one's performance when shooting at big-game animals. One of the most basic elements is which eye is used when aiming the sights. Each of us, assuming we have two functional eyes, has one eye that is considered dominant over the other. For ease of shooting, it's important that the dominant eye be used to aim. Thus, if the right eye is dominant, the shooter would normally shoulder a rifle from the right side, for example.

Unfortunately, sometimes one's dominant eye doesn't correspond to which hand is preferred for fine-motor tasks. So, it's possible that someone who writes (and would prefer to shoot) with his or her right hand, discovers he's/she's left-eye dominant. In this circumstance, it's best to shoulder the gun from the left side, in order to have the head in the proper shooting position, and train the left index finger to pull the trigger. Obviously, the earlier in one's shooting career the dominant eye is identified, the easier it is to make these types of adjustments. I know this firsthand, as I'm naturally left-handed, but right-eye dominant. At a young age, I learned to shoulder the gun from the right side and manipulate the trigger with my right index finger. It is possible to shoot with the non-dominant eye, but it's awkward and requires one to close the dominant eye, limiting one's field of view.

The dominant eye can be easily identified through simple exercises. For example, with both eyes open use a finger to point at a distant object, then close one eye. If the finger doesn't move and it's still pointing at the object, the open eye is dominant; if the finger shifted completely off the object, the closed eye is dominant. Another way to determine eye dominance is to use both eyes to view a distant object through a small opening held at arm's length. Such an opening could be created by placing both hands nearly together, for instance. While continually focusing on the object, slowly retract the opening towards you. You'll discover that the opening naturally migrates to the dominant eye.

In order to shoot well, it makes a difference whether or not one's body is pointed at the target. Obviously, I'm not talking about gross discrepancies, such as when you're positioned facing left when the target is directly in front of you. Rather, I'm referring to subtle misalignments between shooter and the intended point of aim.

As one assumes a shooting position—any shooting position—the body has a place where it naturally tends to point. Referred to as the "natural point of aim," this is the posture where the body is most comfortable and the muscles most relaxed. If the supposed target doesn't happen to be exactly aligned with the body's natural point of aim, strain is introduced to the shooting platform as the sights are muscled from their natural point towards the objective. This muscle tension tends to weaken the inherent stability of the position since the body is, in essence, struggling to hold an unnatural posture. Also, straining muscles, however slight, quickly introduce tremors to the mix; and they reduce the length of time the position can be maintained. Neither of these two things is especially helpful in making precise shots in hunting situations.

So, how do we know when our body is pointing in a natural—muscle neutral—direction? The best way I know is to take whatever shooting position is desired with the eyes closed. Whether standing, prone or sitting, shoulder the gun just as you normally would, but with closed eyes. Once you're settled in and comfortable, open your eyes. If you're able to see the target in the sights, you've assumed your natural point of aim. But if you're skewed to either the left or the right of your target, you need to make an adjustment. The proper way to do this is to shift the entire platform slightly, until the sights and the target are in line. If you're standing, move your feet and not your upper body; if you're sitting, rotate on your butt until you're lined up; and if you're shooting prone, change the direction the body is pointing. The aforementioned adjustments in shooting position are really only applicable to misalignments in the horizontal plane. Vertical discrepancies must be compensated for by other means, such as lengthening or shortening the legs of shooting sticks or bipods.

Many hunters, especially those with limited experience, aim and fire without retaining a specific recollection of the sight picture as the gun discharges. If asked whether the shot was "good," they're frequently unable to say with any certainty. In contrast, the best marksmen can immediately offer a general location for the shot, relative to the intended point of aim. For example, they can reliably predict whether any particular shot will hit too high, or left of the desired impact point. They also know when they've executed a poor shot.

This ability to recognize where the sights were located just as the trigger is released is referred to as "calling the shot." The development of this skill is a testament to the shooter's concentration and trigger control, and it signifies that an important threshold has been reached on the journey to becoming a good shot. Once you've developed consistency, and you can routinely predict where the shot will hit prior to seeing the actual hole in a piece of paper, you've mastered the fundamentals of shooting. From that point forward, instead of learning how to shoot, you're refining skills already in hand. Being able to call shots doesn't mean you'll never again make a poor shot, just that you'll be the first to know when it happens.

No matter how accomplished one is, there are always problems that can jump up and damage one's confidence. Equipment failures come immediately to mind. I've had scopes suddenly lose their zero. Once, I even had my muzzleloader go from shooting great one week to unbelievably bad the next. A gunsmith later discovered the rifling was pitted very badly. I'm still puzzled by why there was such a dramatic change in performance from one shooting session to the next. In any event, if you suddenly find yourself in a situation where there's been some marked departure in how well you're shooting, suspect your equipment as being the primary cause. First check the obvious culprits, such as loose action screws and scope mounts, before moving on to more exotic explanations.

Besides equipment snafus, hunters can also find themselves in shooting slumps. Just like baseball players who go several games and can't seem to buy a hit, shooting occasionally has its ups and downs. Although less dramatic than problems related to equipment, troubles that can be traced to the person pulling the trigger are no less frustrating, and they are often harder to fix. What frequently happens is that the struggling shooter has inadvertently allowed some bad habits to creep into his or her shooting form. This tends to occur gradually over time, so that there is no singular event that can be pointed to as having caused the problem. If you find yourself in such a situation, go back to the fundamentals and carefully examine your performance as it relates to each of these items. Hopefully, you'll discover some flaw in form or execution that you can subsequently correct.

Arguably, the most common bad shooting habit is flinching, which can be described as reacting to the gun going off before it occurs. The most common reason for flinching is shooting a gun that produces more "kick" and/or muzzle blast than is comfortable for the person doing the shooting. All of us have a different tolerance for noise and how hard we're willing to have our shoulder punched.

Muzzle report, besides contributing to a tendency to flinch, is guaranteed to permanently damage one's hearing. Obviously, the louder the noise and the more frequently one is exposed to that noise, the greater the likelihood of developing a flinching habit and the more profound the total hearing loss. Therefore, no one should shoot without ear protection, even if using the mildest of noise-makers, such as a .22 rimfire weapon. It's often not practical to use conventional hearing protection while hunting, but in those situations where it is feasible, I recommend its use there also. Relatively new to the market are electronic hearing devices that are supposed to dampen loud sudden noises, such as gun shots, while allowing normal hearing. As of yet, I don't have any personal experience with these contraptions, but I do know they are expensive. In addition, I can't imagine they're ideally suited to all hunting situations.

An increased proneness to flinch also comes from shooting hard-kicking calibers. Long ago, someone smarter than me stated that it's far preferable to shoot a less-potent gun well, than to shoot a powerful gun poorly. In order to be killed cleanly, some game animals require a gun capable of producing a big punch; however, most do not. So unless you're completely unaffected by recoil or you're hunting large and possibly dangerous animals, I suggest using lighter-hitting guns to get the job done. Believe me, you'll shoot more often, be less likely to develop a flinching habit, and you will become a better shot.

Sometimes flinching is hard to diagnose. As a shooter, the only evidence may be an unexplained errant shot, or a significant enlargement of group size. The best way to determine whether flinching is a problem is to have another person load the gun. They can put a live round in the chamber, or not, at their discretion. The shooter won't know when the firing pin will fall on an empty chamber or a loaded round of ammunition. It will be readily apparent if the shooter flinches while executing the shot on an empty chamber, as the head will twitch in anticipation of the gun discharging, approximate to the trigger being released.

Muzzle brakes are a relatively new phenomenon on hunting guns. They were developed to make potent calibers more pleasant to shoot. While it's true that brakes effectively reduce felt recoil, they do so by trading some recoil for increased muzzle blast. In my view, if the goal is to become a good shot, it's not a trade worth making. If you can't handle the recoil generated by a particular cartridge without acquiring a flinching problem, you're better off searching for a less-powerful chambering. Swapping a shoulder pounding for more noise is not advised, as both contribute to flinching.

There's another bad shooting habit that I call "peeking the shot." Sometimes, in our eagerness to see the effects of a bullet we intend to launch, we prematurely look to see how the animal reacted before the trigger pull is completed. Of course, bullet placement is no better than if one had flinched, but the causes for failing are different—as are the treatments. Whereas flinching is caused by fear of bodily pain and shows up in practice sessions, peeking normally occurs only when shooting at game and is caused by a lack of concentration. Therefore, peeking is easier to treat. Simply being aware that this malady can pop up in hunting situations can serve to redouble one's focus on executing a good trigger pull, maintaining one's form until well after the bullet has left the barrel, and avoiding any urge to look for the effects of tissue damage until the first two items have been completed.

A discussion of shooting mechanics may not generate the same excitement as other topics, but a working understanding of this subject and the acquisition of the underlying skills forms the foundation on which true shooting ability is built. If one is to become a good shot on big-game animals, it's essential that the fundamental elements of shooting technique be understood and subsequently incorporated into the shooter's form. A gun sporting a responsive trigger and manageable recoil is important to the development of shooting skill, and to the avoidance of bad shooting habits, such as flinching. Real shooting prowess comes once the trigger finger becomes intimately familiar with its counterpart, and when the person holding the gun can make it discharge at the precise moment when the sight picture is ideal.

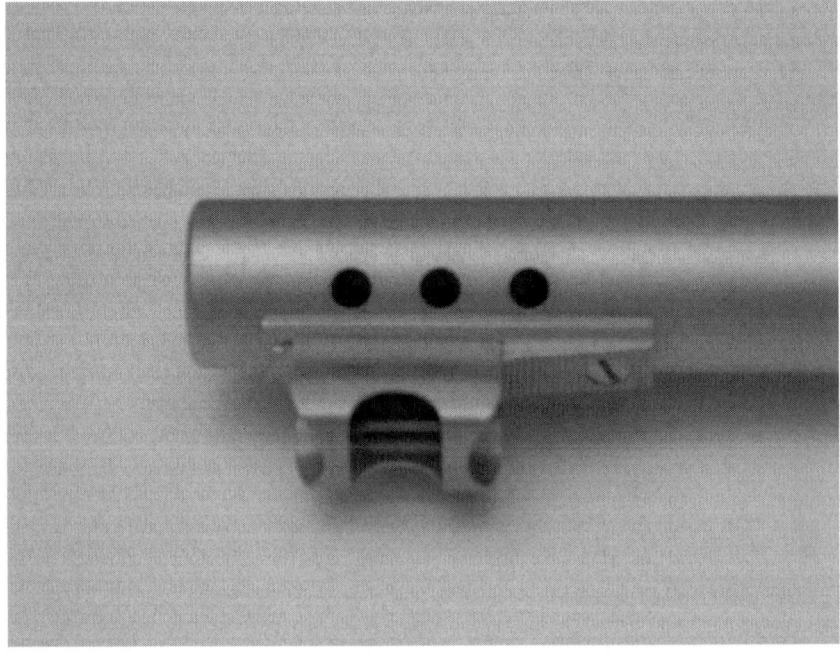

A rifle with a muzzle brake. Porting the muzzle reduces felt recoil but increases muzzle blast, which can lead to bad shooting habits, not to mention hearing loss.

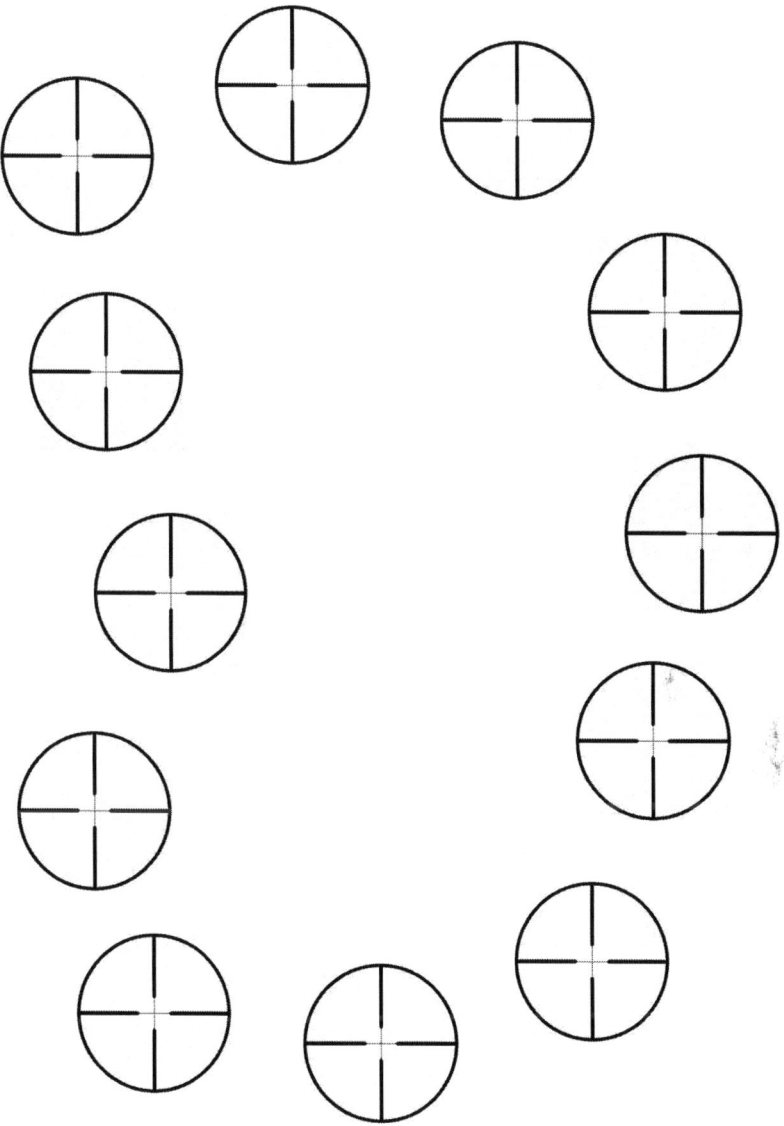

Learning to effectively deal with sight wobble is an important skill to acquire. Intimate familiarity with the gun's trigger is essential if the shot is to broken just as the sights reach the ideal position.   *Images courtesy of Leupold*

Shooting from a surfboard would be unsteady in the extreme. Hunters would do well to develop the most stable platform available to them whenever they anticipate shooting at game animals.
Photo by Cpl. Megan L. Stiner, courtesy of U.S. Marine Corps

STEADY OR NOT

There's a huge difference between the shooting routinely seen at the practice range and shooting at animals in most hunting situations. At the average rifle range solidly built benches are available. If you choose, you can then add sand bags or some other mechanical rest to further immobilize your gun. To be sure, this kind of set-up has its place in the development of good shooting technique. But when's the last time you saw an animal killed from this steadiest of shooting configurations? I can't recall such an occasion either, though some of the elevated buildings I've seen whitetail deer shot from on television come pretty close.

For those of us who do the bulk of our hunting on our feet, it just isn't feasible to slog along a portable bench rest—if such a thing even exists. Therefore, we must resign ourselves to the fact that our shots will likely be taken without the comfort and stability afforded by a well-built bench and bags. And if we are to succeed, it's essential that we attain a high degree of proficiency in those shooting positions that are available to us in the field.

I think it's fair to say that the majority of big-game animals taken with firearms are shot from the ground by hunters using a field position of some kind. These positions include standing without support (off-hand), sitting, kneeling and prone. All can be made steadier by incorporating external supports and stabilizers, such as shooting sticks, bipods, trees, rocks and rifle slings. Let's examine the various possibilities and combinations, evaluate their relative steadiness, and make suggestions about when and where they may be of practical use to hunters.

OFF-HAND

The least stable of all the shooting positions is off-hand. Yet, off-hand shots account for numerous big-game animals each year, mainly because this stance is frequently used by hunters pursuing whitetail deer—which just happen to be North America's most plentiful and hunted big-game species. Although off-hand isn't a very steady position, it does offer the hunter a high degree of maneuverability. By simply turning and bending at the waist a hunter can adjust point of aim significantly. If need be, the feet can be quickly and quietly repositioned to provide even greater horizontal latitude when preparing to shoot. This capability allows one to easily aim at anything in the field of view. In addition, standing upright offers the hunter a high vantage point from which to see over obstacles such as high grass and low shrubs. For these reasons, off-hand is a favored position in the whitetail woods where it's thick, the shooting distances short, and the action rapid. Because of its lack of stability, though, even the most proficient of off-hand shots wouldn't recommend this position for shooting distances much in excess of 100 yards.

If time and circumstances allow, a standing position can be steadied significantly by utilizing objects, such as nearby trees, for support. Just be careful that the gun doesn't directly contact the tree, as bullet flight could be adversely affected by the bounce between two hard objects (gun and tree) that can occur on recoil. A simple solution to this problem is to place the hand supporting the gun against the tree, so the gun itself doesn't contact the tree.

A regular rifle carrying sling can also be used to solidi-

The off-hand shooting position. Although it's the least stable position, off-hand offers advantages of flexibility and speed of deployment. Photo by Janet Carter

fy an off-hand shooting position. Hold the gun in your shooting hand, letting the sling droop towards the ground. Place your support hand through the opening between the gun and sling, going from outside towards the inside, leaving the back of the upper arm to contact the sling. Separate the shooting and support arms until there is tension on the sling. Then, rotate the wrist upward towards your face until the inner aspect of the wrist contacts the sling. Next, rotate the hand over the sling and grasp the stock in the normal support position on the gun's forearm. Slide the support hand along the stock and towards the body until there is no slack in the sling. When finalized, the sling should provide tension at the back of the upper arm, the pinkie side of the wrist and the back of the hand. In addition, the non-shooting hand and sling should be capable of fully supporting the gun in a normal shooting position. The upper body should feel substantially stabilized when compared to the same position without the use of the sling. To get the most benefit from the sling, it may be necessary to adjust its length slightly for fit. And, the optimum sling length for shooting purposes may differ from that deemed best to carry the gun on the shoulder.

Those hunting in Africa rely substantially on standing positions from which to take shots. Most African game is taken at relatively short range, and usually in the presence of significant underbrush. Therefore, upright positions are preferred. While pure off-hand shots are often used for very close shots, especially on dangerous game, the more commonly used variation incorporates tall shooting sticks for increased shooting stability. I'm sure shooting sticks would be as welcome in the whitetail woods if it were practical to pay someone to schlep them along, as is the case in Africa.

Three-picture sequence illustrating how to use a carrying sling to steady a shooting position. First, the non-shooting hand is placed through the space between the gun and the sling, from outside towards the inside. Second, with the sling resting against the back of the upper arm, the non-shooting hand loops around the sling before gripping the stock. Third, the non-shooting hand is retracted towards the shooter's body while gripping and supporting the stock. When completed, the sling should contact the back of the upper arm, the inside of the wrist and the back of the hand.   Photos by Janet Carter

SITTING

Sitting is a significantly more stable position from which to launch bullets than is off-hand. Granted, anyone can sit down and shoot a rifle, but the key to squeezing the maximum stability from a sitting posture lies in how the upper body makes contact with the lower body. Generally speaking, the elbows come in contact with the knees. But it's important that the point of the elbow not rest directly on the knee cap, as this configuration isn't very solid due to bone-on-bone contact. Instead, the backs of the upper arms (triceps muscle) should rest across the inside aspect of the upper and lower legs where they meet at the knee. This positioning is steadier because the contact surfaces are broader and flatter, and because the arm muscles provide a natural cushion that isn't possible when two bones are touching. The legs can be crossed at the ankles or not, depending on circumstances and personal preferences, and the body is pointed approximately forty-five degrees off the intended point of aim. For a right-handed shooter the body would point to the right, while a lefty would be positioned forty-five degrees left of the target. Vertical adjustments to aim can be accomplished by raising or lowering the legs, either individually or in combination.

The unsupported sitting position. Notice that the upper body makes contact with the lower body via flat surfaces of the arms and legs, and not at the bony points of the elbows and knees.   Photo by Janet Carter

Unfortunately, hunters who are older or "flexibility-challenged" may find it difficult to scrunch down into an effective sitting posture. In addition, once one is "locked" into a sitting configuration and aiming at an animal, there is little latitude to make adjustments—especially in a horizontal direction—before it becomes necessary to move and start anew. If an animal moves significantly, it may be impossible to shoot towards this new location without repositioning oneself. Severe uphill shooting angles can present problems in adopting a good sitting position, mainly because of the feeling that you might tip over backwards. This could actually happen, at least on recoil, given a sufficiently high center of gravity on the shooter's part combined with a gun that's a potent kicker. However, downhill shooting lends itself very nicely to sitting, as visibility is normally good and adjustments are easier to make.

Stability of the sitting position can be further enhanced by use of a sling, or by incorporating either shooting sticks or a bipod of appropriate height to support the firearm. It's also possible to use natural features, such as rocks, logs and trees, to accomplish the same thing. As before, it's important not to rest the rifle barrel or stock directly in contact with another hard object. To do otherwise risks experiencing an errant shot. With shooting sticks and bipods there's usually enough dampening of recoil—intrinsic to the device and/or between the shooting aid and the ground—that rifle bounce is of little concern. However, it would be prudent to prove this assertion at the practice range with one's chosen shooting aid before accepting this statement as fact. Even then, in an extreme circumstance, such as when resting a bipod or shooting sticks on solid rock, bounce might cause a shot to fly high. So, practice shooting off rock to see what effect, in any, can be expected on bullet placement.

When using sticks or a bipod, the shooter is positioned noticeably more upright than when assuming an unaided sitting posture. Thus, in addition to being more steady, shooting with these aids is more comfortable and better lends itself to those with diminished flexibility. As before, connection between the arms and the legs will add stability, but my previous warnings regarding point-on-point contact of the knees and elbows should be heeded. The shooter's body will still point roughly forty-five degrees from the direction of aim. When using an aid to shoot while sitting, I find that in most circumstances I can develop more sturdiness with my legs apart, with my forward leg placed between the two legs of the shooting aid. Of course, variations in topography and shooting angle may dictate some improvisation on the shooter's part, in order to achieve the most stable shooting platform for the situation.

The sitting position using shooting sticks. This posture is somewhat more upright than an unsupported sitting position, and therefore more comfortable.
Photo by Janet Carter

High grass, brush, rocks and trees can all interfere with one's line of sight, and preclude the use of a sitting position while hunting. In most circumstances, it takes some time to assume a solid platform on one's backside. Therefore, sitting doesn't work well for shots that are unanticipated or those that need to be taken quickly. However, in situations where the hunter is not particularly rushed, sitting is an excellent position from which to take game. Examples of such scenarios include: spot-and-stalk hunting and stand hunting near well-used trails or waterholes, conducted in places where the terrain is reasonably open.

Just how far one can effectively shoot via any particular sitting position can't be exactly spelled out. Certainly, range can be expected to be extended beyond what's possible from shooting off-hand. Ultimately, though, one's maximum range becomes a function of how steady any particular platform is, and whether an individual hunter is practiced and capable in that situation and at that range. For some, 400 yards may be realistic in good conditions. Those with less talent, or skilled hunters in less than optimal conditions, might need to limit their range to half that distance. Extensive practice will help develop a feel for which shots can be taken, and those which should be deferred.

KNEELING

Kneeling is a somewhat odd position from which to shoot. On one hand, it's only slightly steadier than off-hand, but doesn't demonstrate the same advantages of visibility and maneuverability. On the other hand, kneeling raises one's head only slightly compared to sitting, but isn't nearly as steady. Consequently, kneeling can be thought of as a hybrid position, but without significant advantages over either of its parents. That may account for the fact that, at least in my experience, kneeling is very seldom used in real-world hunting situations. I know I've never attempted a shot at an animal while kneeling.

Having thrown a lot of cold water on the use of kneeling for hunting purposes, I can envision situations where its use would be preferred over standing or sitting. For instance, suppose you're behind a rock that blocks your view of an animal while sitting, and you don't have the luxury of moving. Suppose also that the shot is just beyond your capability while shooting off-hand, and standing upright will likely expose too much of yourself, causing the animal to spook. Kneeling behind or beside the rock just might steal the little extra visibility you need to aim without frightening your target, and the rock might provide enough stability to enable you to make the shot.

In such situations, most of the time it's possible to either change your location slightly or wait for the animal to move, so you can assume the more desirable—and steadier—sitting position. My previous hypothetical example really falls into the realm of improvisation, which I'll spend more time on later. Kneeling is used so rarely in hunting situations, I can't justify devoting time at the range towards its mastery, as there are more important skills that need to be developed and maintained.

PRONE

Prone is another position noted for its intrinsic stability. In fact, for most hunters an unsupported prone position is preferred over its sitting counterpart, all other things being equal. For most people, prone is an easier stance to adopt than is sitting. When assuming a prone posture, the shooter will be on their belly with their body pointed about forty-five degrees off the point of aim, similar to when sitting. The legs are comfortably spread apart. Most of the gun's weight is supported by the elbow of the non-shooting hand, which rests on the ground. The elbow of the shooting hand also rests on the ground and helps steady the position.

Prone, like sitting, requires some time and effort to assume. And, it shares the same limitations in adjusting to changes in target position that hamper sitting. Shooting on level ground is suitable for prone, as are shots taken at uphill angles. As the angle increases, however, the possibility of cuts to the eyebrow area grows also, due to the diminishing distance between scope and head. At significant downward angles, it becomes difficult to shoot from prone, as gravity works to make the position feel less secure. Of course, a prone posture can only be utilized in the absence of significant vegetation or other obstructions, which serve to block the shooter's line of sight. Therefore, prone is only routinely applicable to open-country hunting.

The prone position using a sleeping pad to support the rifle. Notice the body is angled approximately 45 degrees from the direction of fire.

Photo by Janet Carter

As with all shooting positions, the use of a rifle sling can further enhance the inherent sturdiness of the prone position. It is very common to use some external method of support when shooting from prone. Coats, rocks and logs can all be put into effective service, and on short notice. However, the most popular external means of gun stabilization, by far, is one of the many commercially available bipods. By using a bipod, especially one with legs that can be adjusted for height, the front of the gun becomes immobile and the non-shooting hand can assist in stabilizing the butt. The result is, arguably, the most steady field position obtainable. The use of shooting sticks is not practical when shooting prone, however. As with sitting, the maximum range at which shots should be attempted from prone depends upon the shooter's demonstrated ability at distance and in comparable circumstances.

IMPROVISED SHOOTING

No matter how practiced and proficient you may be hitting targets from the conventional shooting positions, you can bet on one sure thing while actually hunting: Sooner or later, and maybe much more frequently than that, it just won't be possible to fit into any of these textbook stances when the opportunity to shoot comes. You could find yourself squirming among large rocks, where you either can't get your legs out of the way or can't get them to support your elbows. Alternatively, after determining that no other positions are sufficiently stable, you may find you're able to perfectly steady your gun in a prone posture, only to discover you can't quite see your target. There are unlimited variations on this theme, all of which are frustrating and can cost us animals.

So, what do you do when you find yourself entangled in one of these unfortunate scenarios? Quite simply, the best you can! Your best asset at times like these is your brain. You must continue thinking and searching for something innovative or novel that fits the circumstance. What you can't do is panic. And if you are unable to ultimately piece something together that provides a platform steady enough to take a shot with a high level of confidence, you can wait for another opportunity that does. That's a far wiser course of action than risking a miss and sending the game out of the country, or worse yet, wounding an animal.

When exposed to trying situations, it's wise to be as logical as possible. If you were to consider the shooting positions you're familiar with as tools in a toolbox, try to see if any particular tool fits the circumstance better than the others. Then see if that tool can be altered slightly or augmented to accomplish the task. If you're unable to see over some obstacle, stack rocks or sit on a backpack as a means of elevating your line of sight. If you need to support an elbow with a knee, which you can't quite move to the right spot because of the topography, consider placing a piece of clothing (or two) between the joints.

Sometimes it's necessary to think "outside the box" in order to find a satisfactory solution to a problem. For example, you and your guide are returning from a day of hunting when you stumble into a nice mule deer just before dark. The deer's already looking at you 125 yards away, ready to bolt. You have a bipod suitable for sitting, but if you sit you'll lose sight of the deer. The only shot you're going to get must be taken standing and quickly, but the range exceeds your ability. What would you do? One solution would be to shoot using your guide's shoulder for a rest. That's safe as long as due caution is exercised in assuming and exiting the position, and the muzzle is well forward of your guide's head when shooting. The guide can cover his ears with his hands to protect his hearing, and still use his elbows, abdomen and legs to lock his body into a fairly stable platform. You would have both hands and the guide's shoulder to steady the gun.

I'm pretty sure you would find the steadiness provided by this arrangement superior to that of a pure off-hand shot, allowing you to take—and make—what would otherwise be considered a very marginal shot.

No matter how creative you may be in the field, you must resign yourself to the fact that sometimes, no matter what you try, your shooting position won't be as solid as you'd like or you're used to. At this point, you're faced with a choice: take the shot or turn it down. Only you can decide, but your decision should be based on an honest self-assessment of your ability. In my opinion, that judgment can only be made by evaluating how well you shoot in similarly unsteady situations while practicing. And if you only practice from rock-solid rests, you really have no experience to draw upon, and no business taking such a shot. So, devote significant practice time to shooting in less than ideal positions and conditions. You'll be glad you did.

SHOOTING AIDS

I've already covered how shooting aids, such as slings, bipods and shooting sticks, can be used to strengthen the various positions one can shoot from. In this section, I intend to discuss particular products in terms of their features, in order to give the reader some guidance regarding their applicability in the field under various hunting situations.

First, it's important to note the differences between bipods and shooting sticks. Shooting sticks are free-standing devices that aren't directly attached to a firearm. In the hunting vernacular, the term "bipod" traditionally referred to a two-legged shooting aid that attaches to the rifle stock, usually via the front sling stud. At the present time, there is some overlap in language which might cause confusion. For example, there are aptly named products called bipods that are free-standing. At the same time, because they have three legs, there are products advertised as tripods—some of which fas-

Improvised standing position using another person to provide support, Notice that the support person's ears are covered and their head is well behind the muzzle.   *Photo by Janet Carter*

ten to a gun and some stand alone. Since the overwhelming majority of products that connect to firearms have two legs, I'll continue to use the term "bipod" for these aids—no matter how many legs are present.

As we've just seen, shooting sticks can have up to three supporting legs. The most rudimentary shooting stick is a stout tree branch or sapling, although commercial monopods are available. The multi-legged versions have some means whereby the legs connect to each other near the top of the apparatus, such as with bolts or heavy rubber bands. Typically, when one is preparing to shoot the gun rests just above this point, either on a small cradle or between the uppermost stubs of the legs. When not in use, the legs pivot about their connection for easier carrying. In addition, some models have legs that are telescopic, or can otherwise be broken down to simplify their transport.

Most often, shooting sticks are employed when a hunter is either standing or sitting. Obviously, the length of the legs must be matched to the expected use and the hunter's physical dimensions, as a standing position necessitates longer legs than does a sitting position and all hunters are not the same height. Shots taken while standing require legs approximately 50-65 inches long; sitting shots need shorter legs, in the range of 20-30 inches. The height of most multi-legged products can be finely adjusted by altering the position of the legs in relation to each other. Moving the legs further apart lowers the height, while bringing the legs closer together elevates the shooting platform slightly. Before buying any particular product make sure it fits your frame, or can be adjusted to do so. In almost all cases, a hunter will use the support hand to steady the sticks and the firearm when shooting. That's the main reason shooting sticks aren't practical when shooting from prone.

Bipods are most often used to augment prone and sitting positions. Standing positions are less suitable for bipods because of the awkwardness and weight involved in carrying such a large support system attached to the gun. However, I do know of one manufacturer that makes a bipod with a quick-disconnect feature, allowing one to transport the support legs separate from the firearm—much like shooting sticks—then rapidly reconnect the legs prior to shooting. The height requirement for the legs of bipods used for sitting and standing is comparable to those needed for shooting sticks. Bipods used for shooting prone have legs in the neighborhood of 9-13 inches long.

Many bipods feature spring-loaded legs that can be deployed instantly and lock in place when activated from their normal carry position parallel to the gunstock. Models containing legs that are independently adjustable for height are helpful in producing stability on uneven ground. Many products have the ability to swivel, pan, tilt or cant about their mounting system, to one degree or another. The most versatile models provide substantial latitude for aiming adjustment in all directions.

For my money, if I had to choose between shooting sticks and a bipod, I would select the bipod. Let me explain why. Shooting sticks normally require the hunter to use their supporting hand to steady the sticks and the gun. Otherwise, the gun could potentially slide on the sticks towards or away from the shooter, or the sticks themselves could shift—especially those with two legs. Either of these eventualities could ruin a shot. With a bipod the legs are firmly attached to the gun, which automatically precludes movement of the gun relative to the supporting system. In addition, since the non-shooting hand is no longer required at the gun/stick interface, it's free to be put to use wherever and however it may be most useful in steadying the shot. That place may be on the rifle stock with the elbow resting at the knee in a sitting position, or under the butt of the gun when shooting prone, to list just two possibilities.

Bipods have one additional capability that recommends them over shooting sticks. When not being used, a firearm can be set on the ground, but in a manner that protects the gun from falling and incurring damage. Combined with the bipod's legs, the heel of the gunstock forms a very stable three-point stance which can help prevent accidents.

The bottom line for me is this: in most hunting situations, bipods are easier to employ, and all other things being equal, offer a more stable shooting position when compared to their free-standing counterparts. Keep in mind that individual hunting circumstances may dictate a different conclusion and another choice.

I encourage everyone to carefully evaluate the conditions that can be expected while hunting and the features of the various commercial products, prior to selecting a tool. It's quite possible that one shooting aid won't prove satisfactory across all hunting conditions. If that's the case, there's nothing wrong with having different aids for different types of hunting environments.

No matter which specific gadget you choose for your hunting, there are a couple of points worth considering. First, it's important that you spend sufficient time shooting from the aid prior to taking it hunting. Such practice should include quickly deploying the contraption and getting into shooting position. Second, whether shooting sticks or bipod, it's vital that the feet of the legs be firmly planted before shooting. Otherwise, they may disengage and slip, causing a missed shot. This is more crucial with two-legged models where the legs are placed at angles approaching, or greater than, ninety degrees to each other; or where the legs contact surfaces that don't hinder the feet from sliding, such as smooth and/or wet rock.

So that you can better appreciate the types of considerations that should go into selecting a shooting aid, let me relate my choice and the reasons why. I do a fair amount of sheep hunting in the mountains, using a spot-and-stalk approach. I own a bipod that I use for these hunts. Specifically, I own a product called the SnipePod, made by Kramer Designs Corporation, which is designed for shooting while seated. The SnipePod system uses a semi-permanent piece that attaches to the forward sling lug, but the legs are removable. When a shot is expected, the legs can be quickly connected to the hardware left on the sling lug. The other features of this system include: a head which joins both legs, each of which operates independently in a ball-and-socket configuration; legs made of hollow aluminum tubes, and in sections connected by a shock cord, much like tent poles; and a mechanism on the head that locks the legs down when shooting, but permits the fully deployed legs to fold against the stock for ease of carry. These features make for a light, portable tool that is highly flexible in its application. The legs can be independently placed almost anywhere, and the ball-and-socket connections allow tremendous latitude in aiming.

My rationale for choosing this particular product and model is multifaceted. First, backpack hunting in the mountains is very strenuous, and every pound you carry matters. This product, carrying case and all, weighs less than eight ounces. Second, most shooting done in these environments is not rushed. There's usually plenty of time to set up the shot on unsuspecting animals. That allows me to carry the legs in my backpack most of the time—where it's easier—and not on the gun. If I'm on a final stalk, I can attach the legs but fold them along the stock, where they're out of the way. Third, I chose a model designed to be employed while sitting, because sitting is a commonly used position for this type of hunting and terrain. In addition, although I fully anticipate the need to shoot from prone on some occasions (where my bipod would be useless), I assume I can develop that stance from other material I have on hand, such as my backpack, items of clothing, etc.

There is only one rule that must be adhered to when shooting at big-game animals: Always shoot from the most stable position possible! It's not a sign of weakness to use shooting sticks to help steady a standing shot; it's an indication of intelligence. Hopefully, this chapter has provided insights regarding how to develop strong shooting positions; and how to strengthen those positions with external devices, such as slings, shooting sticks and bipods, in order to further enhance our ability to make accurate shots in often difficult circumstances. By incorporating these methods and tools into practice regimens, we can become better shots on game. And in the end, greater skill and steadiness when shooting translates into more success as hunters.

This is a bipod for shooting from the prone position. This particular model has the ability to cant, and features legs adjustable for length. The legs stow forward against the stock when not in use.

My SnipePod shooting sticks and case.

Nature's monopod. If there's enough time, a nearby tree can be used to help steady a standing position. Just be sure that the gun doesn't directly contact the tree, as an errant shot could result.   *Photo by Janet Carter*

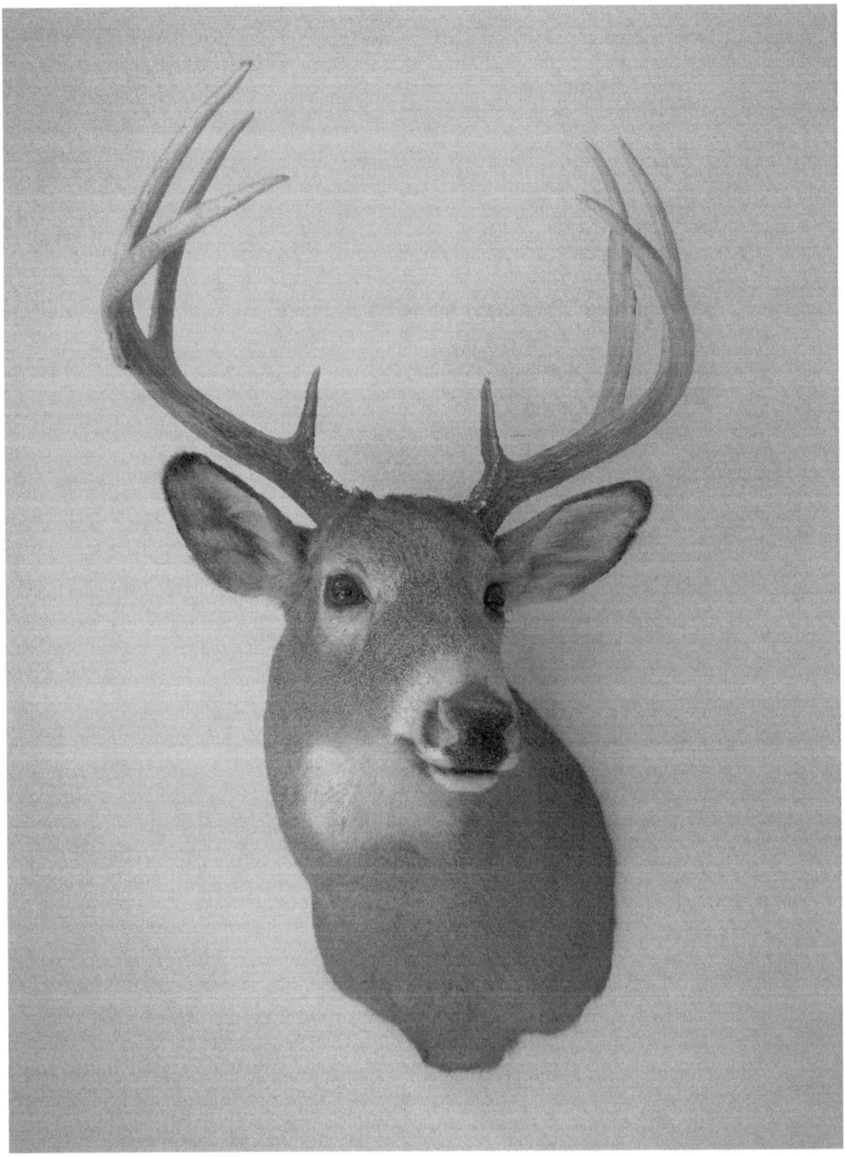

When presented with a shot opportunity, it's much wiser to concentrate on the task at hand and not look forward to how great the trophy will look on the wall at home. Otherwise, you could lose your concentration and subject yourself to a major disappointment.

MIND GAMES & MENTAL TOUGHNESS

There are shots we occasionally miss and then there are, well, embarrassingly bad missed shots. I'm talking about blowing shots that seem so simple you really can't believe you actually failed to connect. Take it from me: failing at the "piece-of-cake" shot is a hurt that lasts a very long time, especially if the animal is grand. From my own experiences and those passed along to me by others who've faced similar despair, I believe most of these types of miscues can be attributed to shortcomings in mental preparation or discipline. Rushing, failing to concentrate and overconfidence are but three of the more common faults originating with the mind, rather than technical ability. Throw in all the additional botched shots caused by the inability to effectively deal with the expected emotion that accompanies a shot at a big-game animal, and you can appreciate that mental weakness is ultimately to blame for a great many bullets that should find their mark but don't, even though the shooter is otherwise capable.

It's important to start with the understanding that no person can be 100% successful at anything, no matter how skilled or prepared he or she may be. Human beings aren't machines and we aren't perfect. As an example, consider professional basketball players. Free throws, otherwise known as foul shots, are the simplest of offensive tasks in the sport. When taking free throws a player stands a mere fifteen feet from the backboard (the front of the rim is even closer) with no one guarding them. Yet even the best at this aspect of the game still miss at least 5% of their attempts. Those who are less accomplished miss more often. Additionally, all players tend to miss these shots at a higher rate as a particular shot's importance to the outcome of the game increases.

There are similarities in the arena of big-game hunting. No matter how proficient one is at the range or during practice sessions, misses will occur there, as well as when hunting. More errant shots can be expected while in the field. This is primarily because there are infinitely more variables that can be thrust upon the hunter while pursuing game, compared to the relatively controlled environment of the practice range. In addition, just as in shooting free throws, as the personal value or importance of a given animal to a hunter increases, the tendency to miss the shot rises also.

This last sad truth has nothing to do with external influences, and everything to do with what's going on between your ears. Internal, self-generated pressure can be triggered by a long drought or a string of bad luck while hunting, because the animal has exceptional horns or antlers, or because the hunter has a natural tendency to get excited when in the presence of big game. Whether we call this phenomenon "buck fever" or some other term, its effects can be debilitating and deflating; and it must be effectively dealt with if we are to enjoy success. Don't mistake my meaning. I'm not saying you shouldn't become excited when in proximity to big-game animals, just that the thrill of the moment not be allowed to overwhelm higher thought processes. After all, if seeing these creatures and anticipating a shooting opportunity doesn't send your heart rate higher, I suggest you give up the sport. Hunting should be thrilling; that's what keeps us out in the elements when it's bitter cold or snowing sideways, and even when we're dead tired.

So, we can expect excitement when close to our quarry—that's normal. But we need not dissolve into a bowl of gelatin. The goal is to control our emotions, maintain our physical and mental capabilities, and execute a good shot. To help illustrate what's at stake and how we can better manage our emotions, let's examine a couple of realistic but vastly different hunting scenarios, and analyze the likely effects on the typical hunter.

In the first hypothetical example an elk hunter has been glassing from a good vantage point for a couple of hours without seeing any animals. There's other good elk habitat nearby that can't be seen from this position, so the hunter decides to move further up the ridge so some of this hidden cover can be glassed. As the hunter approaches this new position, he peers over the ridge into a previously hidden basin and immediately spots a bull elk with his naked eyes, less than 100 yards below him. He quickly shoulders his gun and shoots, dropping the elk in his tracks. Only then does he notice his hands shaking and his heart beating rapidly. In this circumstance the hunter really didn't have much time to think about the impending shot and his reactions were primarily instinctive, rather than cognitive, in nature. The hunter's skills, developed through repetitive training, were able to operate without interference from the conscious brain and he made a good shot. Only after the shot did his emotions come to the forefront.

In the second scenario another elk hunter will have a dramatically different experience. Again, our hypothetical hunter is glassing, but this time he spots a nice bull from across the canyon. The elk is much too far away to take a shot, so the hunter decides to move closer to his quarry. After an hour of carefully and quietly picking his way towards the bull, he arrives at a rock outcropping about 200 yards from the animal. He can't possibly move any nearer without being detected, but he's very confident taking a shot at this range. The only remaining problem is that the bull is now bedded and all that remains visible is its head and antlers, which happen to be the largest our hunter's ever seen in the wild. The hunter must wait until the elk rises from its bed before he will have a clear shot. Unfortunately, that isn't going to happen before four excruciating hours have passed.

Of course, the hunter has no way of knowing exactly when the bull will get up, so he must maintain constant vigilance so he doesn't miss his chance. Further complicating matters is the uneven ground and less-than-comfortable position our hunter must deal with in order to stay hidden, as well as the added impact of the cold temperatures compounded by the long period of inactivity. As if these physical impediments weren't sufficiently challenging, our hunter must also deal with the mental consequences caused by staring at that great six-point rack for those four seemingly interminable hours.

As much as the first scenario could be described as quick, simple and reactive; a perfect conspiracy of circumstances has turned the relatively routine shot faced by the hunter in the second scenario into a long, complicated and contemplative ordeal. The chief difference between the two situations is clear. In the latter case, before a shot can be fired, the brain will have had four long hours to wander, anticipate, second-guess and stir doubts. Unchecked, the mind can wreak havoc on judgment and acquired fine motor skills—if steps aren't taken to control negative or unproductive thoughts.

Let's allow that anyone would be severely tested by the conditions faced by our second hunter. However, the obstacles to executing the shot are still primarily mental in nature, as the elk has a fairly large "kill zone" which provides for a wide margin of error, and the shot is well within our hunter's capability—at least at the practice range. But our hunter most definitely isn't at the practice range and the situation he faces is far from normal. In fact, he may have never been in a similar circumstance before. So, when the bull finally stands up is our hunter going to make the shot? The answer depends, at least partially, on how stable a rest he can cobble together from the items he has on hand. Of much greater importance is his ability to "keep his cool" while under the stresses of his present situation, and then calmly make the shot when the opportunity arises.

Fortunately, there are specific strategies and techniques that can be employed to suppress undesirable and unhelpful mental pressures which might ruin a shot that is otherwise within one's capabilities, and help make an encounter with a big-game animal end with satisfaction, instead of disappointment. The real goal is to force the logical part of the brain to control the emotional side.

Let's begin with those techniques which can be incorporated into practice sessions and will help develop the ability to perform in stressful situations, before we return to our fictional hunting situation. When shooting at the range there are no live animals present to tease or excite us, and no forced waiting before a shot can be taken. The atmosphere can be described as decidedly non-stressful. But, there are things that can be done to artificially mimic the more difficult conditions found while hunting.

I believe it's important that one become skilled at consistently hitting targets from field positions before increasing shot difficulty with any of the following tactics. But once one has developed true proficiency while shooting in unpressured environments, artificial stressors can be added to practice regimens. For example, you can easily elevate your heart rate before taking shots. Simply running in place or up an incline just prior to pulling the trigger will approximate your body's likely physiology when seeing an animal in the field. Any observers who are nearby may think you've lost your mind, but this exercise provides realistic practice in executing a good trigger pull with your heart pounding and with the attendant increase in wobble of the gun's sights about the target. Initially, you can expect your shots to stray noticeably compared to shooting with a normal heart rate. But with continued practice, you should be better able to master your body and keep your shots grouped within an area constituting the vital zone of whatever animal you are hunting.

As a means of demonstrating what's possible in this regard, consider the biathlon. The biathlon is an Olympic sport that combines two seemingly incompatible activities—cross country skiing and fine marksmanship. The participants are required to hit targets immediately after a leg of strenuous skiing. Somehow, these athletes must quickly calm their pounding hearts, steady their bodies and execute good trigger pulls as the clock ticks. Through a combination of mental concentration, breathing exercises and relaxation techniques, these athletes are able to function under extreme conditions. Hunters can do likewise, with proper practice and preparation.

While hunting, the goal is to reduce mental pressure. While practicing, however, striving to increase mental pressure can prove beneficial to our performance in actual hunting situations. Again, I don't recommend any of the following techniques until real prowess has been developed shooting from field positions. But once that has occurred, you can artificially elevate the importance of some of your practice shots. This can be done in several ways. Assigning a significant monetary value to a shot is one such mechanism. For instance, betting your hunting buddy $100 (or whatever denomination you deem suitable) you can make a particular shot adds additional pressure to your shooting technique. Naturally, the greater the inherent difficulty of the shot, the more pressure you'll tend to experience. Similarly, you may want to include your spouse in your shooting sessions. Let him or her name a penalty you must pay if you miss a specific shot. If you truly believe an errant shot on your part will cost you money, a distasteful chore at home or something else of value, you'll feel much more pressure than when simply pulling the trigger unfettered by any external influences.

The ability to concentrate is a valuable skill for a big-game hunter to possess. This skill can be enhanced during practice sessions, also. Ask someone to walk around behind you, talk to you, or otherwise attempt to distract you while you shoot. You won't be able to shoot accurately unless you can completely tune out the distraction and focus entirely on your shooting technique.

The aim of all these exercises is to increase concentration, control emotion and properly execute to your full potential in difficult, pressure-packed situations. Just remember to keep things fun. You needn't alienate a friend, ruin a marriage or go broke trying to become a more proficient and disciplined marksman.

Now that we've discussed some of the practice regimens that can be used to prepare for hunting situations, let's return to the second fictional elk-hunting scenario. Let's examine what can be done in the field, while waiting and immediately prior to shooting, to improve the chances of making a good shot on the bull once he finally stands.

First, understand that one's mind is going to spend the intervening hours between sighting the bull and pulling the trigger doing something. Our job is to consciously control what the brain considers during this interval, so that when we do shoot, our state of mind is as focused and confident as possible. That sounds simple enough, but it really isn't.

Let's start by enumerating the types of thoughts that should be quelled at all costs. Any thinking that gravitates to past failures or missed opportunities must be suppressed. Dwelling on past negative outcomes is a recipe for present disaster. Equally detrimental are thoughts that take us ahead of the actual task at hand, such as imagining how jealous (or proud) your friends are going to be back in town when they see your trophy, or how great the mount is going to look on your wall. In fact, I believe the more you can do to avoid any thoughts regarding horn or antler size, the better off you'll be. Focusing on how good or desirable an animal's head is puts unnecessary pressure on the shooter and distracts from the immediate task.

Instead of recounting past mistakes or leaping to the future, one should be entirely focused on the here and now. That means putting the time you have before actually firing a shot to good use—preparing yourself for the specific job of executing that perfect sight hold and trigger pull. The first task is using your body, the local environment and whatever else you have at hand to construct the most stable shooting platform possible under the circumstances. That's a subject addressed in detail elsewhere in this book. The second task is to mentally log all the individual items that will have to be taken into account prior to executing the shot. Where do I want the bullet to strike? What is the distance to the target? Do I need to account for a significant uphill or downhill angle? Is the wind going to be a factor? Are there objects, near or far, that could possibly interfere with the bullet's path to the animal? These are all questions that need answers before a shot can be taken. Even the simplest of things, such as making sure there's a round in the chamber and the safety has been disengaged, need to be considered and planned for before shooting, or the result could be disastrous. Don't laugh! Many hunters have lost animals because they forgot to perform these most basic of steps.

Once a mental checklist of variables that need to be considered and planned for is completed, you can begin to mentally rehearse your actions leading up to and through the completion of the shot. This is called visualization and it can be a powerful tool to help calm nerves, build concentration and confidence, and maintain control of your body's musculature. The idea is to experience, through your mind's eye, a specific chronology of events culminating in a successful outcome. Such a mental sequence might proceed something like this for our hypothetical elk hunt: You imagine the bull rising, reminding yourself to wait until you have an unobstructed broadside shot; you see the cross hairs on the pre-selected aiming point of the bull's chest; you flip the safety off and steady the gun while consciously controlling your breathing; when the sight picture looks perfect you carefully pull the trigger; and then you see the elk stumble and subsequently fall.

The more detailed your imagery and the more often you run through this mental dress-rehearsal, the more practiced, calm and prepared you will be when faced with the real-life opportunity. It's also advisable to anticipate some slightly different variations on the main scenario, so you don't lock yourself into visualizing just one process. For example, the elk may not stand in a clear opening long enough to take a good shot, or you may not have a legitimate shot until the elk has moved farther away, or the elk's presentation turns out to be quartering rather than the hoped for broadside view. It can be extremely helpful to have mentally prepared for likely contingencies and calculated in advance whatever adjustments would be necessary to meet other potential realities. The lack of such flexibility can cause panic when events don't play out exactly as you may have projected, and that's never helpful.

Constantly playing and replaying an impending shot like this helps keep your mind from gravitating to negative thoughts or doubts, keeps you focused on the immediate task of executing the shot, and helps build confidence because of the positive imagery. However, four hours is an extremely long time to have to wait to shoot at an animal. Shorter waiting times are preferred. For however long one must defer pulling the trigger, though, visualization can be employed to control emotions and calm nerves. Even when a hunter has very little time to prepare for a shot, this exercise can be compressed to fit the available time. If you're well-practiced and proficient, it really only takes seconds to run a mental checklist of factors that need to be considered, make the appropriate decisions and rehearse a sequence of events before breaking the shot. You can also employ visualization during practice sessions. It's just another way of making practice more realistic. Then when you're facing an actual opportunity while hunting, the entire process will seem natural and routine.

As a tool visualization has limits. I've addressed its use in the context of shot opportunities that are definitely within one's abilities. Shots which are clearly beyond one's capability should be considered differently. After all, how do you visualize a shot you know is well beyond your effective range, one where your chance of making a clean kill is minimal? In this context, trying to employ the power of positive thinking is little more than wishful thinking; and big-game animals are too magnificent to be trusting bullet placement on the answer to a prayer. Having said all that, we've all faced situations where a particular shot is at, or just beyond, our known capability. Maybe it's late in the day and waiting for that perfect broadside shot isn't an option, so you must try and thread a bullet to a portion of the vitals; or the animal's just a little too far away, but it's impossible to close the distance; or the wind is blowing significantly stronger than you would like and you're not sure how much your bullet will drift. I believe the decision to shoot under marginal circumstances, as well as the consequences, falls entirely on the person with their finger on the trigger. But once a decision to shoot is made, it should be attempted with as much confidence as possible. That means using any and all tools at our disposal—including visualization and positive thinking—to help us execute the best shot possible.

When faced with a potential wait before you can shoot, such as with our second elk hunter, there's a strong temptation to rush things before the animal gets away, or to convince yourself that you can thread a bullet through obstacles and hit a small portion of the animal's vitals. After all, the animal is right there and well within range, so your brain whispers to you, "Let's get the job done!" It's important to avoid this tendency to rush headlong into immediate but marginal opportunities. This urge is just another way for your brain to force you into action, so it won't have to deal with the mental pressures that will ensue if you decide to wait. Stay disciplined and wait for a good opportunity.

I once missed a Rocky Mountain bighorn sheep because of this kind of impatience. The animal was bedded within range and I elected to shoot at the reduced vital area that posture presented, rather than wait for the larger target (and easier shot) a standing animal would have given me. It's been almost fifteen years since that episode, and I still regularly recount those events and kick myself for rushing my shot. But I did learn something from the experience, however painful it was.

In hunting situations where you're within range of an unsuspecting quarry, time is almost always on your side. The smart play is to wait for an unobstructed shot at an animal's entire vital zone, whatever the angle, rather than succumbing to the immediacy of a tempting but marginal window. Of course, that usually means waiting for the animal to stand up, move several yards or turn slightly. And when you finally do get the shot you want, don't be afraid to back off and regroup if the sights aren't immediately steady or you're not as composed as you would like. Just take a few extra seconds to settle yourself into the shot before pulling the trigger. You must have the mental discipline to avoid shooting when the sight picture isn't good, whatever the reason.

Like the circumstance where one must wait before shooting, there are other situations where a particular shot is within one's expertise, but other factors conspire to make the shot seem more difficult or nerve-wrenching. For example, hunters from the eastern portion of the country who hunt in the western states are very often intimidated by the open nature of the terrain that exists there. Even if they are supplied with the exact distance to a target animal and they know the shot is within their capabilities, some will still let the lack of vegetation convince them the shot's more difficult than it actually is. Similarly, hunters who are used to shooting on relatively flat terrain are routinely spooked when shooting at significant uphill or downhill angles, even at distances at which they are proficient. To be sure, there are real ballistic considerations when shooting at angles from the horizontal, but the simple lack of familiarity with one's surroundings can be a serious impediment to performance. Recognition of this reality is an important first step in overcoming the problem. As before, consciously forcing the logical portion of the brain to steady and control the emotional side is the key to peak performance while hunting. After all, if you can make a 150-yard shot at home with no difficulty, you can make a shot of the same distance with open space surrounding you, or at an uphill angle. You simply have to convince yourself that the target is still only 150 yards away, and the shot is well within your abilities.

There's another important component to remaining calm in actual shooting situations—breath control. When placed in stressful circumstances most people tend to forget to breathe normally. Instead, breathing tends to become either very shallow or irregular. The former case is characterized by rapid breaths that don't fully utilize the lungs, while the latter type exhibits a start-and-stop pattern where air is reflexively gulped when the body can no longer do without oxygen. Both of these unnatural and inefficient methods of breathing can cause feelings of panic, which can, in turn, adversely impact shooting technique.

It's important to consciously control your breathing

when you find yourself under stress, whether hunting-related or not. Simply remembering to breathe will help, but you can accomplish much more by intentionally regulating your breathing pattern and intensity. Slow deep inspirations, then holding for a few seconds before slowly exhaling, then pausing for a few seconds, and repeating this sequence can be quite calming. This type of breathing is commonly called "square" breathing because of the four equal time legs of the exercise, and the eventual return to a starting point. Sometimes closing one's eyes for several seconds while breathing in this manner can further serve to relax the practitioner.

Most shooters are taught breath control as part of good shooting technique. The usual recommendation is to take a full, deep breath and exhale; then take another breath and exhale half of that breath just before pulling the trigger. There's a sound physiological basis for this advice. "Square" breathing is completely compatible with this approach: just release half of the lungs' volume on the exhale leg of the square.

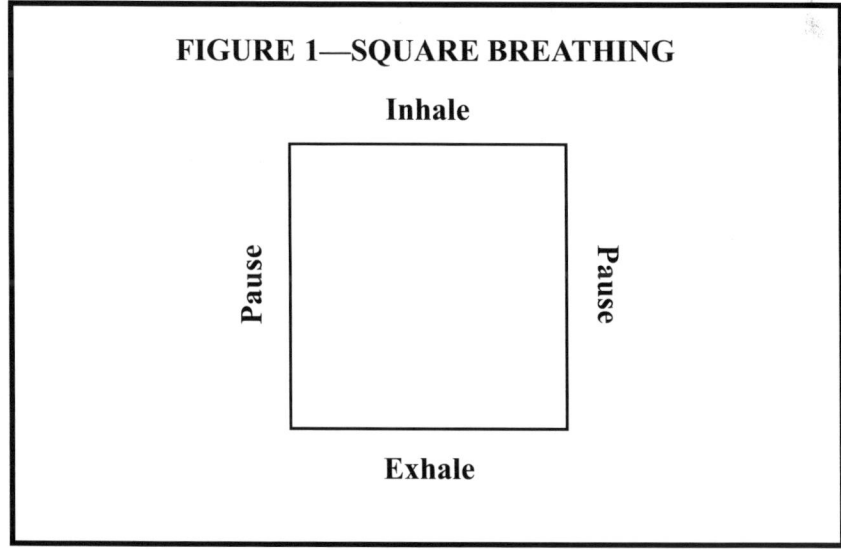

I've spent most of this chapter detailing ways to increase mental control and build confidence. A few cautionary words are in order regarding an affliction that's just as capable of costing us game as self-doubt. Overconfidence is pride run amok and it is to be avoided! When your mindset is such that you feel you can't possibly fail on a shot, there is a tendency to bypass the normal mental checklists, or overlook something which is important and must be considered for the shot to be successful. Thus, you could ultimately find yourself in the position of eating a very large piece of "humble" pie. Approach every shot opportunity, whether ridiculously simple or difficult, with the same attitude. Consider every possible contingency that could affect the shot, remain disciplined and concentrate on execution.

Given this chapter's emphasis on the mind and positive mental control, some may wonder just how important and necessary this subject matter is to becoming a good shot on big game. Some may even consider the whole discussion a bunch of psycho-babble. For the record, I am not a psychologist; I've never even played one on television. However, I have personally used most of the practice tools and coping mechanisms I've described to help get me through some rough spots in my hunting career. Obviously, I believe mind control and mental discipline have an important part to play in hunting success. Whether any reader agrees, or chooses to adopt some, all or none of these suggestions, is left entirely to the individual. In the final analysis, all that's really important is that we make every shot we are capable of making. The specific tools which one finds helpful in attaining that goal are rightfully left to each individual hunter.

The biathlon is a sport that requires participants to make precision shots immediately following the physical exertion of cross-country skiing. Big-game hunters can practice shooting with elevated heart rates to replicate the stressful conditions found when hunting.   Photo by Jack L.Gillund, courtesy of US Army

This is an awkward, uncomfortable shooting position. Since it's often not possible to assume classic—and steady—positions in the field, it would be wise to spend some practice time shooting from odd-ball postures.

Photo by Janet Carter

Effective Practice

If some readers believe real prowess is derived without benefit of knowledge or effort, then I suggest putting this book down. Nothing that follows could possibly be of any help. However, if one accepts as a given the premise that in order to be good at something—anything—one must spend significant time and effort acquiring the necessary skills that particular activity demands, then all that remains open for discussion is how best to obtain those essential abilities.

For purposes of illustration, let's take a small side trip away from hunting to another activity. Consider the game of baseball—specifically, those players swinging bats. Most of us are familiar with the concept of "tee ball," where youngsters new to the game begin by batting stationary balls off an elevated tee. Although this activity is useful in teaching important hand-eye coordination and swing-development skills, it's not truly realistic to the game of baseball, where the ball is moving and hitters don't know in advance where any particular pitch might be located. As players mature, they must face live pitching in order to acquire other essential hitting skills, such as timing the swing and the applicability of the strike zone. So, hitters who hope to perform in actual game situations prepare themselves by taking a lot of batting practice against pitchers who vary their pitches by speed, type and location.

The hunting of big-game animals should be approached in the same way as the previous baseball analogy. That is: the specific shooting skills that need to be acquired for a particular hunt or game species must first be identified, and then practice regimens initiated to obtain those abilities. Practice sessions should be tailored to meet the expected task, mimicking, to the greatest extent possible, the same shooting conditions and circumstances that are likely to be encountered on a particular hunt.

It's important to note that big-game hunting takes place over widely varying habitats and circumstances, resulting in major variations in both the length and types of shots that can be expected. For example, those of us who still-hunt whitetail deer in heavy cover will take most of our shots from an off-hand position at distances less than 100 yards. On the other hand, someone hunting antelope in open country is more likely to be forced to shoot at much longer range, but from the prone position using a bipod. The skill sets for these two types of hunts are similar in some ways, but not identical. And hunters who are comfortable and proficient in one scenario might find themselves completely "out of their element" if suddenly faced with a hunt offering vastly different requirements. Ideally, hunters would develop competency across the spectrum of shot distances and field positions.

For many would-be marksmen, life begins and ends at the shooting bench. Many are quite good shots in this venue and some can be heard proudly proclaiming how they can routinely place three shots inside an inch (or some increment thereof) at 100 yards with their rifle. Fair enough, but does this kind of performance from the bench rest necessarily translate to success in actual hunting situations? The answer is resoundingly—no! Of course, one can be an accomplished shot from the bench and equally skilled on game, but the two disciplines require slightly different skills—and training. However, show me someone who is a crack shot from the various field positions and I'm certain they'll also perform well when given the added steadiness of a bench rest.

The main ingredient a bench-rest practitioner enjoys that a big-game hunter lacks is stability. In conjunction with sand bags or a modern rifle rest, the bench allows the gun to be pointed at the target without human interference or effort. All that's left for the shooter is to make a smooth trigger pull. Hunting situations are dramatically different—and less stable. And unless the hunter can learn to accurately place shots in the field without such rock-solid support, consistent hunting success will be elusive. Unfortunately, today's hunter seems increasingly predisposed to doing the bulk of his or her shooting from a solid bench. Judging by the many varieties of commercial shooting rests available, and the advertisement dollars that are sunk into their promotion, there is a large audience for these products. That's not to say shooting from the bench doesn't have its place in a big-game hunter's preparation. In terms of group size, it's the best place to evaluate how precisely your gun and ammunition performs. The bench is a necessity in adjusting the sights to a specific zero, whether that's defined by so many inches high at 100 yards, dead on at 250 yards, or some other convention. Finally, a solid bench is the best place from which to evaluate sudden performance aberrations in gun or shooter. But beyond these limited circumstances, the bench really has no role to play in making someone a good game shot. After all, you can't take it hunting with you. Therefore, proficiency must be developed from those positions and for those circumstances found while actually hunting. And that can only happen if one duplicates such shots in practice sessions.

Hopefully, I've adequately explained the rationale for doing the bulk of one's practice shooting from field positions in preference to the bench rest. Now, let's consider what to aim at during these sessions. Given a choice, which of the following two abilities would be more valuable to a big-game hunter: being able to place every shot taken in the field into the vital zone of an animal; or being able to consistently shoot two-inch groups on a bull's-eye type target? I expect everyone realizes that animals don't come with bull's-eyes painted on them. Then why do so many of us spend all our time shooting at targets consisting of vertical and horizontal lines or small orange circles and squares? Wouldn't it be more practical—and useful—to aim at facsimiles of the animals we intend to hunt, instead?

I submit that shooting at full-scale replicas of our prey is the best way to go. Here's why. First, every animal has an anatomical "vital zone," which generally consists of the heart and lungs, collectively. Knowing the size and location of these organs—and where to aim so that a bullet reaches them—on various presentations is an essential skill. Shooting at imitation animals forces one to concentrate on anatomy; shooting at geometric figures does not. Second, I've found that conditioning oneself to aim at things like two-inch stick-on squares isn't always helpful in game situations. Although the square is absent on live animals, there's still a tendency to be super-precise with one's aim. In hunting situations where opportunities are often times fleeting, that can be an impediment and cost us game. In addition, in an attempt to be perfect, especially in less-than-steady conditions, sometimes it takes a long time to get the cross hairs to settle exactly where you would like them to be. This delay can be the cause of a poor shot if concentration wanes or muscle tremors emerge as a result of assuming an uncomfortable field position. That doesn't mean the gun can simply be pointed toward an animal and the trigger pulled without regard for where the sights are located. However, once the sights are comfortably located within the vitals, executing a smooth trigger pull is the more important task when compared to squeezing the last inch of aim out of the sight picture. The third reason for practicing on lifelike targets is psychological. On most hunts there are any number of things that can seem foreign or unfamiliar to the hunter. Steep shooting angles and wide-open spaces are two of the more common culprits, but there can be others. If one is used to shooting at targets that appear real, there's one less mental adjustment to make while in the field. That can be comforting and provide a level of confidence that might otherwise be missing. In any event, it's one less adaptation that needs to be made.

Construction of such a realistic target need not be elaborate. I routinely use a piece of half-inch-thick plywood, which I cut into the approximate shape of the animals I intend to hunt. To make such a target, the only information that's needed is an animal's backbone-to-belly measurement and its body length. For example, deer are typically 16-18 inches through the body and about 30 inches from brisket to rump. Antelope-sized game is smaller in both dimensions, while elk and moose are significantly larger. For simplicity sake I don't incorporate the head, but others may find the addition of a head to be more realistic. For legs, I attach two pointed stakes (front and rear) with a couple of screws each. These features allow me to place the target almost anywhere I want, and I can quickly replace a leg should I accidentally break one with an errant shot. I also paint the target to match the color of my expected quarry.

Once constructed, it's time to shoot some holes in the target from field positions. After each shooting session I use a magic marker to outline the new bullet holes, making it easier to identify where the bullets from my next session are hitting. At some point, as holes accumulate, keeping track of additional shots becomes harder. Therefore, I staple a piece of painted paper over the concentration of holes, so I can more easily determine where subsequent shots are striking. This saves me from constantly cutting new plywood. This paper can be periodically replaced as needed. If you shoot enough, eventually the plywood will become chewed up by so many bullets that its integrity becomes compromised. When that happens, just trace the target outline on a new sheet of plywood, cut the outline, paint accordingly and transfer the legs to the new target.

It's ideal to be able to shoot proficiently from all the various field positions. Such versatility is your best insurance against an unexpected—and unpracticed—situation. However, not everyone has unlimited time to hone his or her shooting skills. Therefore, as a practical matter, it may at times be wise to concentrate one's shooting from those field positions that are most likely to be encountered on a particular hunt. For example, let's say you're booked for an African plains-game hunt. How should you prepare? To be honest, I've never hunted in Africa. However, from everything I've seen and read, although the distances aren't great, the vast majority of shots are taken either off-hand or standing using tall shooting sticks. Therefore, if I had an impending hunt in Africa, you can bet I'd do most of my practice shooting utilizing these two methods at appropriate yardages.

Similarly, if I were gearing up for a mule deer hunt where I could expect shots of up to 300 yards, I would do the bulk of my practicing shooting at similar range. Furthermore, I would take these shots utilizing shooting sticks from a sitting position, a bipod from prone, or some other improvised rest—such as from a backpack laid on a large rock. I would rehearse for my hunt this way precisely because these are the types of shots I could expect while on my hunt. Again, the best way to train for an expected activity is to replicate, to the greatest extent possible, the conditions of that activity in practice.

Assuming one finds merit in my suggestion to do the bulk of one's shooting from likely field positions at lifelike targets, how should expertise be defined? This is not a trivial consideration, for at the root of the matter is one's personal sense of ethics. Most of us can agree that some shots should not be taken, as the chance for missing or wounding game would be too great. However, if hypothetical scenarios were presented to a group of hunters, I'm confident there would be wide disagreement regarding when this point might be reached. Personally, I believe each individual has the right—within the law—to determine which shots should be taken, and those which should be passed up. But such a decision should be based on something other than antler or horn size, and there is an ethical responsibility to deal with the consequences of any poorly placed shot which results in a wounded animal.

Having said all the above, let me offer my standard for measuring proficiency, keeping in mind that my goal is always a clean, one-shot kill of an animal. When someone can consistently place 80% of their practice shots within the vital zone of a realistic target at a specific distance, I consider that level of performance good enough to attempt the same shot—from the same position and under the same conditions—in a hunting situation. Others may choose a different standard; that's okay. Whatever the criteria for proficiency, two things are required in order to make such a judgment. The first is knowledge of the animal's vitals in relation to the target outline. The second is intellectual honesty in evaluating just how well-placed each shot is in relation to those vitals.

Since shooting at realistic targets from expected field positions may be a new concept to many readers, let me offer some suggestions on how to develop these abilities. First, start small. Trying to accomplish too much too soon can be discouraging. Therefore, start shooting at shorter distances in calm conditions, before increasing range. For someone who has done all of their shooting off a bench, that may mean 100 yards is the best starting point using shooting sticks from a sitting position. As skill and confidence are gained, target distance can be increased in twenty-five or fifty-yard increments. Once expertise is acquired shooting from one position, start anew from other likely field positions. The object is to gradually increase capabilities over the spectrum of stances and at increasingly longer distances.

At some distance, each of us will "max out" our skills for a particular shooting position. This will be evidenced by our inability to keep enough of our shots in the vitals. For me, that means fewer than eight vital hits out of ten tries. This is important information, as it serves to define the types of shots that can be used while hunting. For instance, you may discover that a shot in excess of 80 yards should not be taken off-hand, and a more solid position, such as sitting or standing using a tree for support, is warranted. One thing is certain: As one's effective range is increased, shots at shorter distances seem increasingly easier to make, whatever the shooting position. And usually, practicing at or near one's maximum range will best serve to maintain those hard-earned skills.

Shooting at significant angles from the horizontal is common in many hunting locales, especially in mountain settings. Shooting at vertical angles introduces two considerations that don't come into play when taking shots on the level. One is ballistic in nature; the other psychological. The ballistics of inclined fire is covered elsewhere, but everyone would benefit from some practical application of the subject prior to an impending hunt in undulating terrain. The mental adjustment needed to comfortably move from shooting on level ground to steeper inclines is significant. Shooting from far above (or below) your target looks different and feels different than when shots are taken on the level. Adapting to such an unfamiliar, and often uncomfortable, circumstance can be greatly facilitated by practice. Unfortunately, unless you also happen to live in or near settings that offer natural vertical relief, it's also one of the more difficult of conditions to imitate in practice, especially for those of us who can be labeled "flatlanders." Nonetheless, if you reasonably expect to take shots at vertical angles during an up-coming hunt, it would be well worth the effort to do at least some shooting from an elevated perch before that hunt. Places where sand and gravel is being extracted, stone quarries and the like can serve to provide the desired changes in elevation, assuming permission can be obtained and the shooting conducted in a safe manner.

One of the most frequently encountered hunting conditions is shooting in significant wind. Yet, very few hunters even know how a particular wind (direction and velocity) will affect the flight of their chosen bullet. Fewer still ever bother to try and actually hit a target when the wind is blowing. Most consider a windy day a poor time to go shooting. After all, the thinking seems to go, the size of my groups might get bigger. Well, of course, you can expect larger groups in windy conditions. You may not even be able to hit the target! But what rational person thinks an unpracticed hunter can suddenly, with a real animal standing 300 yards away, make a lethal shot in a fifteen-mile-per-hour crosswind? So if you expect you might be hunting in wind—and rare are the hunts without wind—then you better know how wind influences bullet flight, how to judge wind speed and direction, and be able to estimate what sight corrections should be made so bullets end up hitting the vitals. This kind of expertise can only come from extensive shooting in windy conditions. Because of its importance and the amount of information that must be conveyed, I've elected to give the subject of shooting in wind its own chapter.

To this point, all the practice shooting I've been advocating involves the use of guns and ammunition suited for whatever big game one may be hunting. And while I believe there's no substitute for such training and that it should constitute the bulk of one's preparation, that's not to say that important skills can't be developed with milder recoiling—and cheaper—rounds, such as .22 caliber rimfire ammo.

While the .22 is ill-suited for long-range work, it is ideal for learning to shoot off-hand, where shots are rarely taken in excess of 100 yards. In reality, it's not even necessary to shoot that far with the .22. Assuming an animal has a vital zone approximating eight inches in diameter, the same degree of difficulty encountered by trying to hit an eight-inch target at 100 yards can experienced by shooting at a four-inch target placed 50 yards away. Of course, the ultimate purpose is to develop the shooter's ability break the shot as the sights wobble about the target.

Some hunting styles involve the need to quickly shoulder, aim and fire a weapon—sometimes at moving game. Tracking or still-hunting whitetail deer comes to mind. In such situations it's important to be particularly smooth in one's footwork and in shouldering the gun. Mere seconds are available for target acquisition. Again, the .22 is entirely suitable for perfecting these motions and skills, without the expense and attendant recoil of centerfire ammo.

It goes without saying that if one is to develop as a shooter and hunter it is necessary to practice. Unfortunately, I can't suggest a specific number of rounds of ammunition that must be fired or how many hours must be devoted each year to become skilled, as individual starting points and goals vary greatly. Besides, true progress should be measured by the attainment of newfound ability and not merely in rounds expended and hours invested. While I don't believe there's any such thing as too much practice, it's unrealistic to expect major advancements in mere days. Instead, longer time-horizons, often measured in years, are the norm for major gains, especially those near the upper limits of one's ability. For instance, it took me a couple of years to extend the effective range with my open-sighted muzzleloader from 200 to 250 yards. Remember, slow and steady often wins the race.

I do think it's more advantageous to shoot a handful of

rounds regularly, than to fire scores of ammo on a few occasions. Thus, five rounds once a week would be preferable to fifty shots fired four times a year. The reasons for this recommendation are simple. First, regular practice helps develop the necessary muscle "memory" of the trigger finger. Absence may make the heart grow fonder, but it also causes a lack of familiarity. Second, it's easier to apply one's full concentration over shorter periods of time. Very few of us could honestly say the fiftieth round of a shooting session would get the same attention as the first. Finally, shooting high-powered rifles over an extended period of time can put the hurt on one's shoulder. Consequently, the likelihood of developing a flinch increases in proportion to the number of shots fired per sitting.

In general, any serious hunter could be expected to invest many hours and fire hundreds of rounds of ammo each year maintaining or improving their shooting abilities. Just how one goes about spending that practice time can affect the ultimate level of skill obtained, and how long it takes to acquire that skill. Practice regimens geared towards replicating expected hunting situations are the most productive means of becoming a good game shot. Ultimately, when faced with real animals in real-world hunting situations and shooting positions, such practice provides the greatest comfort level when one is confronted with a tough shot. And maybe more important than that, realistic practice gives each of us a greater appreciation of our true abilities, helping us to make informed decisions about which shots we can make and those which should not be attempted.

A solid bench can be used to sight-in guns, but the bulk of one's practice should be done using those field positions that are likely to be available while hunting.
Photo by Janet Carter

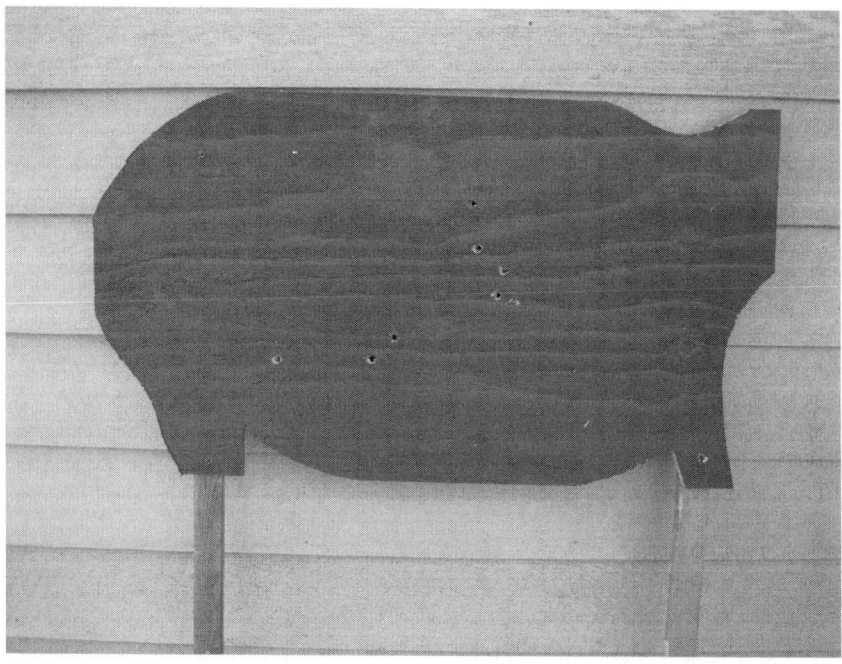

My plywood practice animal. This particular one measures 18 inches from back to belly and approximates the form of a wild sheep.

The shooter's clock for evaluating wind direction. With the shooter positioned in the center and firing towards twelve, any wind present can be described in terms of direction by using an hour-based convention.

Shooting in Wind

For the big-game hunter, it's often true that the best—and sometimes only—opportunity to take an animal comes at relatively long range and in the presence of significant wind. Just how prepared a hunter is to deal with such situations and how practiced they are shooting with wind present may very well determine the outcome of the hunt.

Being able to regularly and accurately place bullets in windy conditions is a significantly harder thing to accomplish than when shooting in the absence of wind. Much needs to be considered in order for a bullet to hit its mark. In actuality, there are three distinct problems associated with shooting in windy conditions, all of which work to degrade the shooter's performance.

First, wind alters the flight of bullets. Referred to as drift, bullets will deviate from their expected path in accordance with the wind's direction and velocity. Wind directions perpendicular to the bullet's line of flight will cause the most drift for a given wind velocity, and are called "full-value" winds. Thus, assuming someone is located at the center of a watch with the target designated to be at the "twelve o'clock" position, winds from the "three o'clock" and "nine o'clock" directions are considered full-value winds and will cause the most drift when compared to a wind of like speed blowing from another, so-called "partial-value," direction, such as from "two o'clock" or "ten o'clock." Direct headwinds and tailwinds ("twelve o'clock" and "six o'clock," respectfully) can be ignored for drift. Of course, the higher the wind's velocity the more drift one can expect, regardless of wind direction. In fact, a wind having twice the speed of another wind, but blowing from the same direction, can be expected to double the drift of a given bullet at any yardage.

If a bullet's muzzle velocity and ballistic coefficient are known, ballistic software will readily calculate the actual bullet drift (usually in inches) at various ranges for a specified wind speed and direction. This information forms the basis of how to deal with wind in the field. Bullets having higher ballistic coefficients and started at faster initial velocities are less affected by winds than are slower, less-efficiently designed specimens (See Table 1).

TABLE 1—WIND DRIFT IN 10MPH CROSSWIND (inches)

Range (yards)	A	B
100	0.77	1.20
200	3.19	5.32
300	7.47	12.84
400	13.87	24.55

A-Muzzle velocity=2,800 fps, B.C.=.423
B-Muzzle velocity=2,800 fps, B.C.=.266

The second problem caused by wind is that it serves to destabilize the shooting platform, especially for field positions. This is because the wind pushes on both the shooter and the rifle, and it usually does so intermittently and with variable force. Obviously, strong gusty winds are more problematic in this regard than are their lighter-blowing counterparts, but any wind stronger than a light breeze will contribute to positional instability. Hunters in the field can sometimes insulate themselves from this phenomenon, at least partially. If possible, look for a location from which to shoot that is sheltered from the wind, even if requires a slightly longer shot. Alternatively, one can try and touch the shot off during a lull in the wind's ferocity.

Because wind is often inconsistent in both direction and speed, it can be difficult to predict just how much it will affect a bullet in flight, which brings us to the third challenge wind presents a shooter—doping the wind. Hypothetically, let's assume you've done some homework in preparation for an upcoming hunt, and you know a ten-mile-per-hour (mph) crosswind will cause your chosen bullet to drift twelve inches at 300 yards. So when presented with this shot, you simply hold your aim twelve inches into the wind and pull the trigger, right? Not so fast. Although the wind-drift information is accurate and useful, it's still only theoretical. Here's why: it's highly unlikely the wind will blow from the exact same crosswind direction, at a constant 10mph over the entire 300-yard span between you and your target, while the bullet's in flight. In some places along the bullet's path the wind may even be coming from the opposite direction. Besides, how do you know the wind speed is really 10mph, and not 15mph or 5mph?

For all practical purposes, judging the wind's actual effect on a bullet in flight is more art than science. Only by shooting in windy conditions can ballistic information regarding bullet drift be integrated with experience, giving the shooter the appropriate insight into where the correct hold should be. Even then, it's altogether possible to misjudge the wind. Furthermore, a sudden unanticipated change in wind speed or direction (or both) just as the trigger is pulled can negatively impact a bullet's ultimate destination.

So, how does one go about doping the wind? The first step is to develop some sense, in miles per hour (mph), as to how strongly the wind is blowing. This skill is usually acquired from visual clues, such as how noticeably grass is bending or trees are swaying, assuming they're available for evaluation (See Table 2). In some hunting situations these visual clues may be unavailable. Hopefully, by the time a hunter is faced with this reality, a "feel" for the wind's speed has been attained from repeated practice where the visual manifestations of wind are present. Alternatively, it's possible to purchase commercial wind meters like those made by Kestrel® and others. Small, portable and inexpensive, these devices will display the exact wind speed—but only where the meter is located. And that brings us to another difficulty when dealing with wind.

Wind speed, especially on longer shots, may not be constant across the entire distance from shooter to target. For instance, a hunter may be exposed to significant wind while an animal may be standing in a well-protected basin some 300 yards distant. Before shooting, a hunter should look for visual clues regarding wind speed not just at the hunter's location, but also near the animal and every place in between.

The next step is to evaluate wind direction. Just as wind speed is often variable, it's common that the wind won't be blowing from the same direction at all points along a bullet's path. As before, examine any available visual clues to help formulate a judgment. Obviously, for a given wind speed, winds that aren't perpendicular to the bullet's flight will cause less drift than those that are. Just how much less drift can be expected is dependent upon the wind's direction. Winds from the "one o'clock," "five o'clock," "seven o'clock" and "eleven o'clock" directions can be expected to cause roughly half the drift of their full-value counterparts. Similarly, winds from "two o'clock," "four o'clock," "eight o'clock" and "ten o'clock" will cause about 87% of the bullet drift experienced by exposure to the corresponding full-value crosswinds.

As a practical matter, it's reasonable to consider these last wind directions (two, four, eight and ten o'clock) as full-value winds, also. Doing so leaves us with only two wind catagories to consider—full-value winds (100%) and half-value winds (50%).

TABLE 2—VISUAL CLUES TO WIND SPEEDS

Calm	Smoke rises vertically with little drift
5mph	Wind felt on face, leaves rustle and small twigs move
10mph	Leaves and small twigs in constant motion
15mph	Small tree branches move, dust raised from ground
20mph	Large branches and small trees begin to sway
25mph	Large branches in continuous motion, audible noise
30mph	Same as above, only with more motion and noise
35mph	Whole trees in motion, inconvenience felt when walking into wind

Adapted from N.O.A.A Beaufort Scale of Wind Velocity

Ultimately, the goal is to take any available clues regarding wind speed and direction and determine where the sights should be held, using known ballistic drift data for a particular bullet. So, if you feel you're shooting into a consistent 10-mph crosswind and the expected bullet drift is eight inches for the range you're shooting, then the correct hold would be eight inches into the wind from where you'd like the bullet to strike. That's a pretty straightforward analysis. But what would your firing solution be in a more realistic scenario, like this next one?

Suppose you estimate the wind to be blowing from your "two o'clock" direction at a speed that varies between five and ten miles per hour, until about two-thirds of the way to the target. From there forward, you believe the wind isn't a factor because a hill is blocking it. The range is 400 yards, and you know a constant 10-mph crosswind will move your bullet fourteen inches at that distance. First, according to your analysis of the wind, you only need to consider bullet drift over the first 267 yards (2/3 x 400). According to ballistic data, a 10-mph crosswind will blow the same bullet about six inches at this distance. But, the wind isn't blowing directly crosswind and it's not blowing steady at 10mph either. As far as drift is concerned, wind blowing from "two o'clock" has 87% of the value (or strength) as a full-value crosswind blowing from the "three o'clock" direction. Therefore, a 10-mph wind coming from "two o'clock" will move the bullet about five inches (.87 x 6). A wind blowing at 5mph would cause one-half this amount of drift, or two and one-half inches. So, holding 2-5″ into the wind should get your bullet to the correct spot, assuming your wind doping was flawless.

As you can see from the previous exercise, by knowing a few essential facts an approximate allowance for wind can be made. In order to elaborate on the relevant considerations, I detailed more calculations than most readers (myself included) would be comfortable performing in the field. Rest assured, a simpler, more empirical, approach will work almost as well. The key elements for success are: knowing the bullet-drift data for your ammunition and being skilled at judging wind direction and speed. Drift data is readily available and it can be brought along on a hunt for reference. Doping wind, however, is an acquired skill that can only be attained through practice.

Let's redo the last shooting scenario using a different approach. Specifically, let's see what happens when we try and convert the entirety of wind speeds and directions into an equivalent crosswind velocity for the entire 400 yard range, using reason and common sense. We believe the wind is blowing 5-10mph for the first 267 yards from a "two o'clock" direction. Thereafter, wind is not a factor. It seems reasonable (equivalent) to treat these observations as if there were a constant crosswind of 5mph over the entire 400 yards. A quick look at the appropriate bullet-drift data shows the need to hold 7″ into the wind, which compares reasonably well with the 2-5″ of windward hold we calculated earlier. Obviously, I overestimated the overall effect of wind, if only slightly. Still, if I make a good shot I should still get a bullet into the vitals. The advantage of using this approach is that it's simpler—no math is needed.

Let's examine another seat-of-the-pants method for calculating hold, using the same underlying facts. This time, I'll ignore the effects of wind beyond 300 yards (267 rounded up). Next, I'll look up the expected bullet drift in a 5-mph crosswind (3.7″) and in a 10-mph crosswind (7.5″), and then split the difference. Using this approach, I figure the correct place to aim is 5.6″ into the wind. Again, this compares well to a more exacting mathematical calculation but it involves less time and effort.

The truth is: everyone's free to use whatever method works best for him or her in developing a proper hold from bullet-drift data. It's even okay to switch between different methods, as some situations naturally lend themselves to one approach in preference to another. To test the suitability of any system, however, it's necessary to go to the range in windy conditions, guesstimate the allowance for wind, and then shoot to see how well those approximations account for the actual influences of wind. Initially, I suggest this shooting be done from the bench, so only the shooter's wind-doping skills are being tested. Otherwise, the added variable of shooter error is more likely to be in play, preventing an accurate analysis of cause and effect. Only after some demonstrated skill in reading the wind is acquired should field positions be incorporated into the exercise.

There are some general guidelines that will make dealing with wind less cumbersome while hunting. First, the effects of wind can be ignored for shots inside 100 yards. And for most rifles and cartridges, this rule applies to shots nearing 200 yards. Unless you're shooting something especially slow and aerodynamically inefficient—like a muzzleloader or the venerable .30-30—or you're shooting in a very high crosswind, bullet drift will be less than aiming error. Since the vital zones of big game animals are sufficiently large, just ignore the wind in these circumstances and make a good shot.

As I've discussed, bullets with high ballistic coefficients and fast muzzle velocities are influenced less by wind than are those started slower and less streamlined in shape. So if the type of hunting you participate in regularly demands shots in excess of 200 yards, you can minimize the effects of wind—and your need to compensate for it—by selecting appropriate bullets and calibers offering higher muzzle velocities. Fortunately, there is no shortage of rifle calibers or commercially available ammunition that fits the bill, not to mention the additional possibilities afforded the handloader. Even so, at ranges in excess of 200 yards, no matter what equipment we use, bullet drift is a reality that must be dealt with. Obviously, the longer the shot and the stronger the wind, the more critical it is to correctly read the wind and make the appropriate adjustments.

At some point, no matter what equipment is used or how skillful one is at correctly doping the wind, the ability to reliably hit what you're aiming at will diminish below an acceptable level. When shooting in wind, this will necessarily occur at some range less than your demonstrated proficiency in the absence of wind. After all, no one is a better shot in windy conditions than he or she is when it's perfectly calm. It also stands to reason that the more forcefully the wind blows, the shorter one's effective range will be. Only by practicing in windy conditions can a hunter determine his or her maximum range in a 10-mph wind, a 20-mph wind, and so on.

Learning to shoot while the wind is blowing, although not easy, is a very valuable skill to obtain. Then, when faced with that long shot in gusty conditions, you won't find yourself in the unenviable situation of being "clueless," or worse yet, panicked. Instead, you can calmly collect your thoughts, refer to your bullet-drift table, rely on your experience to correctly read the wind, adjust your point of aim and make an accurate shot on that once-in-a-lifetime animal.

Gunnery Sergeant Carlos Hathcock (ret.) receiving the Silver Star on November 12, 1996.
  Photo by Sgt. James Harbour, courtesy of U.S. Marine Corps

LONG-RANGE SHOOTING

What constitutes a lengthy shot is very much in the eye of the beholder. For some, any shot taken in excess of 200 yards may seem to be "way out there," while others might not even break a sweat when shooting inside of 600 yards. Of course, some consideration must be given to what weapon is being used. A hunter equipped with a centerfire rifle sporting a high-quality, twenty-power scope is going to have a different view of this than another hunter who totes an open-sighted muzzleloader, for instance. So we can see that the ultimate determination of "long range" is a function of both ability and the equipment at one's disposal.

Before someone comes unglued, I'm not advocating anything here. I certainly don't promote the indiscriminate throwing of lead great distances downrange, just because it can be done. That is irresponsible. On the other hand, a shot of 600 yards, for example, isn't automatically unethical, either. Maximizing one's effective shooting range is a laudable goal for all of us. The endpoints will vary with the individual. My only purpose is to provide relevant and useful information that will assist those who seek to extend their current skills. When a trigger can and should be pulled is ultimately an individual choice. In keeping with my beliefs and my previous statements, however, no shot should be taken unless there is a high expectation of a clean kill. As stated elsewhere, my personal prerequisite for shooting in the field is being able to consistently place eight out of ten shots in the vitals when shooting the same distance under similar shooting conditions during practice.

But just for fun, let's for a moment consider what's possible in regards to long-range precision shooting. Some readers may be familiar with Gunnery Sergeant Carlos Hathcock. Mr. Hathcock served as a Marine sniper during the Vietnam War. During his service he accumulated an astounding ninety-three confirmed kills of enemy personnel. The actual number of lives taken is undoubtedly much higher, as some kills couldn't be independently verified. Many of these engagements took place at extreme distances, often in excess of 1,000 yards. In fact, Sgt. Hathcock has been credited with one kill at the astonishing range of 2,286 meters. That's nearly one and one-half miles! For these feats and others, as well as additional contributions to country, Carlos Hathcock is an American hero and a legend in the Marine Corps.

Those of us with more ordinary shooting abilities will have to be content with more modest goals. For our immediate purposes, let's equip everyone with centerfire rifles and scopes. In this context, I'm going to define "long range" as any shot taken at a big-game animal that exceeds 400 yards. Although that definition is somewhat arbitrary, my rationale for choosing that particular marker is twofold. First, I really believe that most dedicated hunters have the ability to consistently hit the vitals of a big game animal inside this distance, given sufficient preparation and practice. I also believe that shots in excess of 400 yards begin to press the abilities of most hunters, no matter how committed they are or how much they practice. Second, by using the concepts of mid-range trajectory and point-blank range, aiming is manageable to this range limit, but just barely. For example, referring back to the .300 Winchester round I exploited in the chapter on inclined fire, you may recall the bullet is 17″ below the line of sight at 400 yards using a 250 yard zero. Thus, a shot of 400 yards necessitates elevating aim this much higher than the point of anticipated bullet impact. By knowing an animal's backbone-to-brisket measurement, making the proper aiming adjustment is doable—but not easy. At ranges beyond 400 yards, estimating the correct holdover becomes impractical, as the aiming adjustments are measured in feet, and another means of correcting aim must be employed.

I'm sure there are some readers who read the last statement and are thinking, "Wait a minute, can't we just zero the gun to a longer range, say 400 yards?" That way, so the thinking goes, we needn't be troubled with holdover estimations. That's certainly true and this approach can be used, but doing so introduces other problems that we've been able to avoid to this point.

The concept of point-blank range, which I explained long ago, is a useful aiming tool that gives us the luxury of not worrying about correcting aim over a wide range of potential shooting distances. As you remember, in conjunction with an acceptable mid-range trajectory error, we intentionally zeroed our gun so we could simply hold "dead on" at most ranges. That approach limits the need to adjust aim—or hold over or under—to those situations where we must shoot beyond the pre-determined point-blank range.

If we abandon this method and zero to longer range, we create a situation where aim must now be adjusted for shots taken at shorter distances. For example, for the aforementioned .300 Winchester round zeroed to 250 yards, we find that the bullet is never more than 4″ above or below the line of sight (LOS) all the way out to 300 yards. In other words, this round has a point-blank range of 300 yards, assuming an acceptable error of four inches. But look what happens if we keep all other variables the same and zero this same round at 400 yards. Now, the bullet will be 11″ above the LOS at 200 yards (See Graph 1). So, if we came upon an animal at this distance while hunting (a realistic possibility)

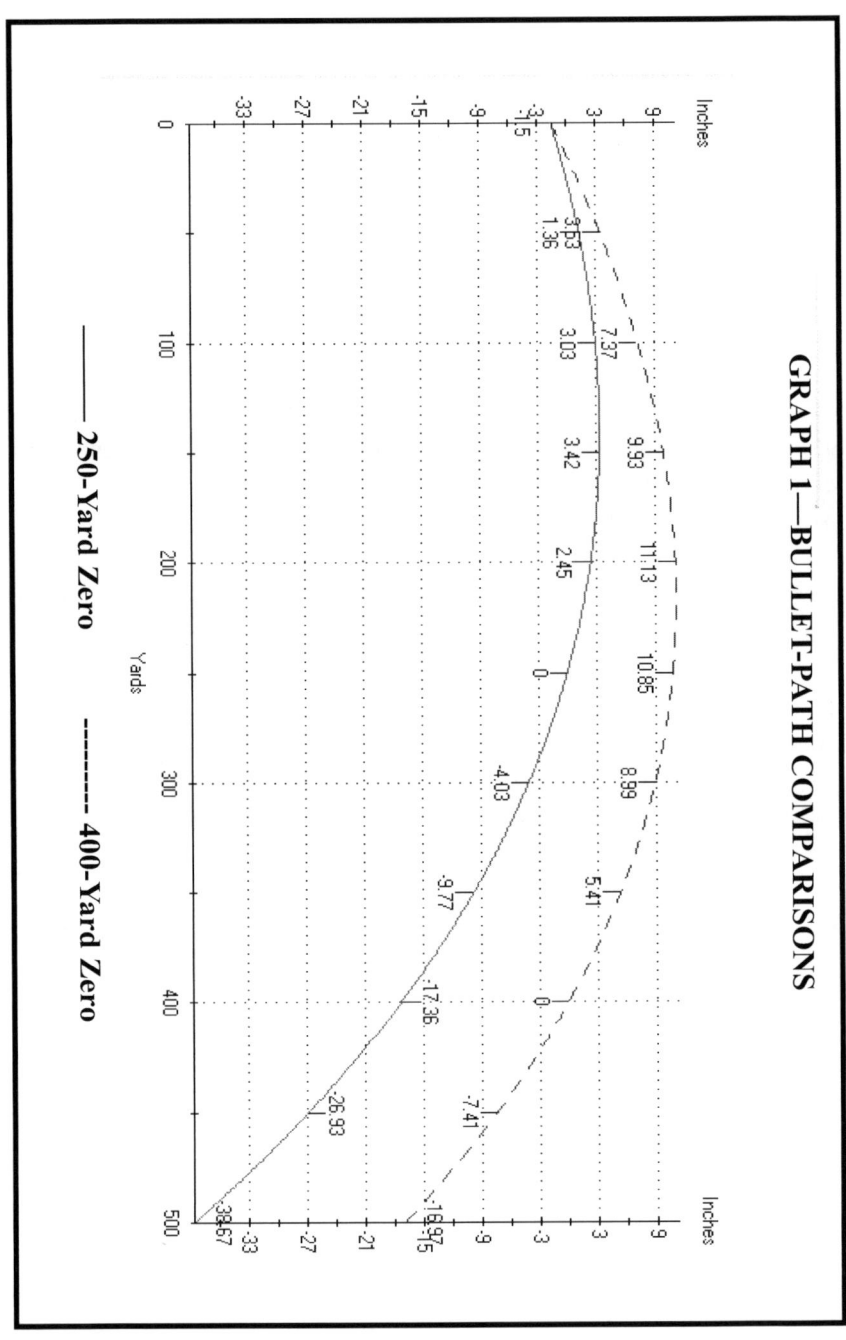

we would be forced to lower our aim accordingly in order to make a good shot. Even at 100 yards, a shot could fly high if the sights weren't consciously lowered. Close encounters with game animals usually leave less time to refer to trajectory tables and carefully deliberate aiming corrections than do meetings at longer range. Therefore, unless the expectation is that all shots will be taken at very long range, I submit we're usually better served by sticking to the "no-thinking" point-blank range approach for close shots and seeking another means of correcting aim for longer shots.

I've detailed the shortcomings of zeroing to long range and the inherent difficulty of estimating holdover at longer shooting distances when the gun is zeroed according to the tenets of mid-range trajectory and point-blank range. Assuming you anticipate the need to take shots in excess of 400 yards or you're at least interested in learning more about the subject, what exactly are the viable alternatives for accurate long-range aiming? In a word, scopes! Actually, there are two different ways a scope can be used for this purpose. One method is intrinsic to the scope's reticle; the other involves using the scope's internal adjustments to correct aim.

SCOPES WITH MULTIPLE AIMING POINTS

If you haven't shopped for a rifle scope in some time, you'd likely be amazed at the array of reticles currently available to the hunting public. Gone are the days when almost all scopes came with simple cross hairs, or some minor variation thereof. Scope manufacturers have developed the ability to incorporate complex reticle configurations into their products, many of which are designed specifically for long-range shooting applications.

Of course, each manufacturer has a proprietary name for its particular reticle. As examples, Zeiss calls its versions Rapid Z®, Nikon™ calls theirs BDC and Leupold® makes the Boone and Crockett™ Big Game reticle (See Figure 1).

FIGURE 1—LEUPOLD BIG-GAME RETICLE

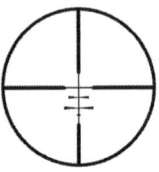

An example of a reticle with multiple aiming points.   *Courtesy of Leupold*

Variations on a similar theme, they all incorporate additional aiming points in addition to the central intersection of the cross hairs. These secondary intersections are comprised of horizontal hash marks, dots or circles positioned along the vertical axis of the reticle, and they serve as specific aiming points for particular ranges in excess of the normal sight-in range. Thus, once the rifle is zeroed at some specified distance (e.g., 200 yards) when the main cross hairs are used for aiming, the secondary intersections become the aiming points for shots taken in excess of this range, usually in 100-yard increments. If a shot of 500 yards is contemplated, the appropriate secondary aiming point is used.

The obvious advantage to such a system is that it provides point-blank capabilities for most shots. That is: there is never a need to hold over or under, at least in theory. For shots up to 200 yards the central cross hair intersection is used; thereafter, another intersection is selected. Occasionally, a situation will present where the shooter must hold between two of the aiming points. For example, when shooting at an animal that is 350 yards distant, one would split the difference between the 300 and 400-yard hash marks.

But, you may ask, what are the downsides to this system? To be sure, there are some. First, some manufacturers provide reticles that are calibrated only to 500 yards. If you expect to shoot farther than that, you've got trouble, at least with a 200-yard zero. And while you certainly could zero the gun at 300 yards instead, that would likely only increase your maximum range another 100 yards. By doing so, though, the secondary aiming points may not conveniently fall at 100-yard increments, as before. In addition, a 300-yard zero potentially introduces problems of excessive mid-range trajectory error.

Second, the reticle system is largely generic. By that I mean it lumps many different calibers and bullets into a single category without regard for an exact muzzle velocity and ballistic coefficient, assuming they all behave identically during flight and print to the same point downrange. As I explained much earlier, that isn't the case and comparative bullet drop and wind drift at a specific range is a function of a bullet's initial velocity and its ballistic coefficient. Any particular bullet and load may not exactly duplicate the generic ballistic model, resulting in error. Moreover, any error that does exist is accentuated as shooting distances grow. So the farther you shoot, the more you must be concerned about your bullet's lack of conformity with the manufacturer's model.

The third area of concern is related to scope magnification. Variable-power scopes are the most commonly used aiming implement in big-game hunting, and they provide versatility across a spectrum of shooting distances. While the central aiming point remains in the same position at all powers or magnifications, the same cannot always be said for the secondary aiming points. For those scopes which have the reticle located in the scope's second focal plane, the secondary aiming points move based on the power setting. To illustrate the problem, consider this: If you were to look through such a scope set on low power with the central aiming point centered on the target, and then increased the magnification to its maximum, you would notice two things. First, the central aiming point would remain fixed in the center of the target even as the target fills more of the field of view. Second, the secondary aiming points would appear to "walk" their way closer to the target's center as magnification is increased. This phenomenon illustrates that the distance each secondary aiming point represents is dependent on the power setting of the scope. Therefore, in order to use the manufacturer's ballistic model, the scope magnification (or power) must be set to some pre-ordained value that is also determined by the scope's maker. If some other power setting is employed, the secondary aiming points will no longer correspond to their advertised shooting distances.

This is not the case if the reticle is located in the first focal plane of the scope. With this design, the reticle's size remains proportionate to the target size no matter the power setting of the scope. In other words, as magnification increases (or decreases), the reticle and the target are enlarged (or shrunk) by an equal amount. Therefore, the secondary aiming points will maintain their values at any power setting. Unfortunately, most variable-power scopes (at least in the U.S.) have the reticle located in the second focal plane, constraining the user to a single magnification value.

Personally, I wouldn't want to rely on a generic ballistic model for precise, long-range shot placement. And, when shooting long range I would most likely choose the scope's highest magnification. Some manufacturers utilize the scope's highest power to calibrate the secondary aiming points; others do not. Assuming your particular scope is a second-focal-plane model that falls into the latter category, but you share my views on generic ballistic models and you expect to use the highest magnification to shoot, there is a solution to both problems. You can customize your scope through extensive shooting. By experimenting with targets set at various distances, an exact correlation of the secondary aiming points to target distances can be made. Thus, when shooting with the scope's magnification cranked all the way up, you may discover the secondary aiming point that the manufacturer suggests be used for shots of 500 yards is accurate for shots of 467 yards using your ammunition. Once you've reworked all the secondary aiming points, you'll have a very useful—and accurate—tool. Just write down the new yardage values for the secondary aiming points, so they can be referenced later.

Finally, whether you customize the scope in this manner or not, once you start shooting along inclines, the range values of all aiming points will no longer be valid. If you choose, ballistic software can be employed to find the differences in bullet paths between the level-fire baseline and various inclined-fire situations. The appropriate adjustments to aim, from the nearest aiming point can be cataloged, and a "cheat" sheet created for use in the field. This can become quite cumbersome and often times confusing, however, as you're necessarily dealing with additions or subtractions (in inches) from multiple aiming points. Maybe there's a better way to shoot at long range, one which avoids all the shortfalls of a reticle sporting multiple aiming points.

USING A SCOPE'S INTERNAL ADJUSTMENTS TO CORRECT AIM

For me, at least, the favored means of routinely shooting at targets beyond 400 yards involves the use of the scope's elevation turret. As you know, scopes can be adjusted in a horizontal direction (windage) as well as in a vertical direction (elevation) via the corresponding external adjustment dials. In fact, we manipulate these dials to get the gun to shoot to the desired point of impact when zeroing the rifle. We can also use the elevation adjustment to compensate for bullet drop on a shot-to-shot basis.

As when using a reticle with multiple aiming points, the rifle is first zeroed at a convenient distance, for example 200 yards. Shots of this distance or less are taken without further adjustments. For shots that exceed 200 yards, the elevation dial is used to compensate for bullet drop. Subsequent to taking such a shot, the elevation dial is returned to its default position. The next time a shot in excess of 200 yards is contemplated, the appropriate correction (whatever that may be) is "dialed in" via the elevation knob. That's the overview, but a detailed explanation is required.

Let's start with the elevation and windage turrets. These days, adjustment of these dials causes movement to the scope's internal parts, and in very precise increments known as clicks. Each click equates to a specific amount of movement, typically expressed as fractions of a minute of angle (MOA). Thus, scopes are often calibrated such that each click corresponds to 1/4 MOA or 1/2 MOA. A MOA is a unit of angular measurement defined as 1/60th of one degree. At a distance of 100 yards this equates to slightly more than one inch. At 200 yards, a MOA would measure a little more than two inches. So, if you want to move a bullet's point of impact two inches at 100 yards and the scope has 1/4-MOA adjustments, it would require eight clicks (4 clicks/inch x 2 inches) to accomplish your objective.

Okay, so we know we have the ability to precisely change where a bullet will hit by manipulating the scope via the windage and elevation dials. Where does that get us, and what else do we need to allow for exacting bullet placement at long range? The only additional information that's required is the bullet path at the target distance. Thus, if the rifle is zeroed at 200 yards and you're contemplating a shot of 500 yards over flat ground, the bullet path for this circumstance would be used to adjust the scope's elevation dial.

Let's go through this process using my .300 Winchester round. When sighted in at 200 yards, the bullet will be nearly 45 inches below the LOS at 500 yards. Therefore, we need to turn the elevation knob so that bullet placement is effectively raised 45˝ at this distance. Obviously, that necessitates following the scope manufacturer's directions, which usually provide arrows indicating up/down directions. Assuming the scope is calibrated in 1/4-MOA clicks, every four clicks will move the point of impact one MOA, or 1″ at 100 yards and 5″ at 500 yards. At 500 yards, 45″ equates to 9 MOA. If 4 clicks equal 1 MOA, then 9 MOA is 36 clicks. Consequently, in order to provide the proper adjustment, the scope's elevation dial must be dialed in the upward direction a total of 36 clicks. Don't forget, once you're finished shooting at this distance, the elevation knob must be dialed back 36 clicks to its starting point!

Counting dozens of clicks for each shot, then subsequently dialing those adjustments back to the original scope setting after shooting is cumbersome and prone to error. It's also problematic that there's often no easy-to-read reference to indicate when the dial is returned to its original zero. Typically, both shortcomings are handled by the use of a custom bullet-drop-compensation elevation dial. These devices provide information in a format more useful to the shooter—yards. So, rather than counting clicks, the hunter simply dials the turret to the expected shooting distance. Return to zero is just as simple, but not absolutely necessary, as you can dial up and down between all practical ranges as the shooting distance changes. But, you must always remember to dial the shot distance into the scope.

Leupold® and others make these custom dials using data specific to a shooter's gun, load and scope. As you may have already guessed, the bullet's muzzle velocity and ballistic coefficient are key. It's also necessary to know the scope's make, model and internal adjustment regimen (i.e., 1/4-MOA or 1/2-MOA clicks) and the intended zero range. Once this information has been supplied, exact bullet-drop data can be generated. Taking into account the expected bullet drop at a given range and the scope's adjustment regimen, a series of precise laser engravings is made on the dials. These marks correspond to specified shooting ranges. Once the new dial is attached to the scope (usually via Allen-type set screws) and aligned so the dial zero (i.e., 200 yards) corresponds to the rifle zero, the shooter can navigate through the spectrum of shooting ranges with a twist of the hand.

A few words of caution are advised. I'm sure you've heard the expression, "garbage in, garbage out." It has application here as well, and the farther you expect to shoot the more important it becomes to input accurate data. Muzzle velocity for your pet load is best measured with a chronograph using your gun. You can reference reloading tables or the ammo manufacturer's data to supply muzzle velocity, but your gun wasn't used to develop the listed muzzle velocities. Consequently, there could be significant variations when compared with your particular equipment. A similar problem exists with ballistic coefficients. There are several scientific models used to determine the ballistic coefficient of a bullet, and manufacturers sometimes supply data that exaggerates the real-life performance of their bullets. The so-called "true" ballistic coefficient of a bullet can be found by shooting and comparing actual performance to that predicted by ballistic software using the manufacturer's stated ballistic coefficient. For example, the software may dictate 39 clicks to hit the target at 500 yards, but actual shooting demonstrates that 41 clicks of elevation are required to hit the mark at this distance. This set of facts indicates the bullet's "true" ballistic coefficient is less than advertised, as there's more than the expected bullet drop that must be compensated for. By playing with the software and adjusting the ballistic coefficient input downward slightly, you should eventually find a ballistic model that matches actual bullet performance. When you have the custom bullet-drop-compensation dial made, just supply the "true" ballistic coefficient, as you determined while shooting, instead of the manufacturer's value.

When it comes to inclined fire, an accommodation will be necessary. As we all should know by now, we can't treat shots taken at angles as though we were shooting over level ground. Consequently, it's inappropriate to simply dial the turret to match a particular slant range when shooting uphill or downhill. Instead, the elevation turret needs to be dialed to whatever yardage mark will compensate exactly for the actual bullet drop that occurs, given the shooting angle and slant range to target.

TABLE 1—BULLET-PATH VALUES (inches)

Range (yards)	0°	30°	45°	60°
200	0	1	3	5
250	-3	-1	2	5
300	-7	-4	-1	4
350	-13	-9	-4	2
400	-21	-16	-9	0
450	-31	-24	-15	-4
500	-42	-33	-22	-8
550	-56	-45	-31	-14
600	-71	-58	-41	-20
650	-90	-73	-55	-28
700	-110	-91	-67	-37
750	-134	-111	-83	-47
800	-160	-133	-101	-59
850	-189	-158	-121	-72
900	-222	-186	-144	-88
950	-258	-218	-169	-104
1000	-299	-252	-196	-123

.300 Winchester magnum, 185 grain VLD Berger bullet, B.C.=.569, 2,800 fps

Since our only available references are the yardage marks on the BDC dial, which were developed for level-fire conditions, let's start there. Using ballistic software, we can convert these marks to the bullet-path values they compensate for. Next, for a specific shooting angle and slant range, we can reference the bullet-path value at the target, again using the software. Now that we're dealing exclusively in terms of bullet-path values, it's a simple matter to search our level-fire bullet-path values for a value which matches that of our proposed shot. Once we've found the equivalent level-fire bullet-path value, all that remains is to convert that value into its yardage counterpart and dial the scope to that yardage.

To illustrate how this is done, refer to Table 1 and follow along. In this case, I've chosen my .300 Winchester magnum utilizing a 185 grain Berger Very Low Drag (VLD) bullet with a muzzle velocity of 2,800 fps. This particular bullet has a very high ballistic coefficient (.569), making it ideal for long-range shooting applications. As you can see, the table gives the approximate bullet-path values at various ranges and angles out to 1,000 yards, in fifty-yard increments. Clearly, the rifle is zeroed on level ground at 200 yards. Let's say we contemplate taking a shot of 550 yards at a 45° angle. The bullet-path value for such a shot is -31 inches. Knowing that, we scour the level-fire column (0°) for an equivalent bullet-path value, which we find at 450 yards. Therefore, we crank our BDC dial to 450 yards before taking the shot.

For ease of use while hunting, we can even take this process one step farther and simply display the yardage the scope should be dialed to for a particular slant range and angle. That way, there's no need to cross reference an equivalent level-fire bullet-path value while hunting. As before, I believe the best course of action is to develop this data beforehand using ballistic software, and create a "cheat sheet" to reference in the field. Figure 2 is such a document,

FIGURE 2—CHEAT SHEET .300 WINCHESTER

Slant Range	15°	30°	45°	60°
200	200	200-1	200-3	200-5
250	235	220	200-2	200-5
300	295	265	220	200-4
350	340	315	265	200-2
400	395	370	315	200
450	440	415	360	265
500	490	460	405	305
550	540	510	450	355
600	590	560	495	395
650	640	605	550	435
700	690	655	585	480
750	740	700	635	520
800	790	750	680	560
850	840	795	725	600
900	885	845	770	645
950	935	895	815	685
1000	985	940	860	730

produced from the ballistic information used in Table 1. The yardage values are rounded to the nearest five-yard interval. I chose to provide data at 50-yard intervals in order to keep things simple. For those who would prefer to reference more exacting information and avoid significant interpolations, the cheat sheet can be constructed using whatever yardage interval is deemed most appropriate.

Depending on the manufacturer of the BDC dial and sometimes on the portion of the dial that's being used, yardage engravings may fall at ten, twenty; twenty-five or even thirty-three yard increments. Therefore, it may be impossible to dial exactly to 265 or 315 yards, as examples, and the closest available range indicator would be used. Notice that wherever there is a positive bullet-path value I expressed the hold in terms of "yardage minus." This reflects the reality that the lowest yardage on the BDC dial is 200 yards, and at that setting the shot will hit high unless further correction is made. For example, "200-5" instructs the shooter to set the BDC dial at 200 and then aim five inches low to compensate for the bullet being five inches above the LOS when it reaches the target.

Using the scope's elevation turret to adjust aim provides several distinct advantages for shooting long range when compared to using a multi-reticle scope. First, the shooter only need be concerned with a single central aiming point—no complicated reticles. Second, there's no need to worry about what power the scope is on—shoot at any magnification you desire. Third, there's no built-in range limitation. Finally, inclined-fire scenarios can be more simply handled given sufficient bullet-path information.

OTHER CONSIDERATIONS

Those who expect to shoot beyond 400 yards often need to be concerned about things that normally are not crucial at shorter ranges. Obviously, the farther the shooting distance, the more important these factors can become. Remaining bullet energy, rifle cant, wind and other environmental impacts are all relevant to the long-range marksman and hunter.

Hunters face one absolute requirement that isn't important for target shooters. To cleanly kill an animal, a bullet must reach its target with sufficient energy and effectively transfer that energy to the disruption of vital tissues. For no matter how precisely placed a particular shot may be, in the final analysis, bullet energy is what's ultimately responsible for tissue damage and death. Assuming the selection of a well-constructed, proven hunting bullet—of which there are many—the question becomes, how much energy is needed to do the job? Well, that depends on the animal and its presentation to the hunter. Speaking in generalities, less energy is needed to kill small, thin-skinned animals, such as deer and sheep, than would be necessary to put down larger, more heavily constructed beasts, such as bears and moose. In addition, broadside shots that need only penetrate lungs require less energy than quartering shots that must plow through substantial tissue before reaching the vitals. While there is no truly objective means of determining sufficient remaining energies for clean kills, there does appear to be some consensus about these matters. Thus, some guidance can be gleaned from the data in Table 2. In the end, the responsible hunter should choose bullets with care, be thoroughly familiar with the capabilities of his or her particular ammunition at every potential shooting range, carefully select which types of shots are to be taken, and use good sense at all times. Only then can wounding or crippling outcomes be minimized.

TABLE 2
MINIMUM BULLET ENERGIES FOR CLEAN KILLS

Deer, Antelope, Caribou, Black Bears	800-900 ft.lbs.
Elk, Grizzly & Brown Bears	1200-1300 ft.lbs.
Moose	1500 ft.lbs.

Another issue that can adversely impact shots at very long range is rifle cant. By necessity, scopes are mounted some distance above the rifle's bore. When shooting, if the bore is positioned directly below the scope, so that the two are in perfect alignment with the direction of bullet drop, no cant exists and the shot should hit where expected. If, however, the bore is rotated about the scope's axis (cant) so they are no longer in alignment with the direction of bullet drop, then a cant error is introduced. This error has a larger windage component than a vertical component, but both exist. The magnitude of the error is dependent on several factors, including the magnitude of the cant angle, the shot distance and how high above the bore's axis the scope is mounted. In addition, cant error can be induced from both clockwise and counter-clockwise canting. From the shooter's perspective, clockwise cants result in shots that hit low and right; counter-clockwise cants leave bullets low and left of their expected placement. Because cant is random, great shot-to-shot variation can occur when attempting to shoot a group. Frustration and uncertainty about gun-ammo performance can result.

So what concrete steps can be taken to eliminate cant errors when shooting? The first requisite is knowledge of the problem. Only then can conscious efforts be made to avoid introducing cant while shooting. Next, it's important to start with a scope that's properly aligned in the scope rings. That necessitates positioning the cross hairs so the horizontal hair is level to the gun when the rings are fully tightened. This can be facilitated by using a product such as the Level-Level-Level made by Wheeler™ Engineering. Properly orienting the scope in this manner helps prevent the inadvertent introduction of cant as one's eye attempts to level misaligned cross hairs. Finally, there are tools in production that attach to the scope or the gun and provide objective evidence that the gun is being held without cant. These items range from bubble levels to micro-electronic devices.

Obviously, the further one shoots the more potential there is for wind to affect any given shot. I've devoted an entire chapter to dealing with wind. Suffice it to say that long-range marksmanship requires highly refined wind-doping skills, as well as substantial practice in windy conditions, before shots should be attempted on game animals. While the scope's windage turret can be used to dial in corrections for wind, in hunting situations it's usually preferable to hold the sights into the wind by an amount necessary to correct for whatever wind is present. Some scopes contain reticles with dots, marks or other features that can facilitate making any necessary aiming corrections dictated by the wind.

Although it will often be necessary to correct for wind, we have some ability to control the magnitude of the needed corrections. We can minimize the impacts of wind by consciously choosing bullets with relatively high ballistic coefficients. As we've seen earlier, such bullets are deflected less by wind than their less-streamlined counterparts. In addition, low-drag bullets better retain energy and exhibit less drop at like target distances. All these things offer advantages, especially as shooting distances grow. For illustration purposes, let's compare two different loads using my rifle chambered in .300 Winchester and zeroed at 200 yards. At 700 yards, keeping muzzle velocity the same (2,800 fps) and shooting into a 10-mph crosswind, a 180 grain Speer spitzer bullet (B.C.=.483) will have a bullet path of -119 inches and be blown off course a total of 41 inches. In contrast, a 185 grain Berger VLD bullet (B.C.=.569) will have a bullet path of -110 inches and display 33 inches of drift. Which round would you rather correct for? In addition, the Berger bullet will still deliver 1,315 foot-pounds of energy at this distance, while the Speer bullet only musters 1,073 foot-pounds (See Table 3).

In our quest for bullets sporting high ballistic coefficients there is one important caveat: terminal performance cannot be sacrificed for the sake of efficiency in flight. After all, we're hunting, and not merely shooting at paper targets. Therefore, it's just as important to choose a bullet that is designed to inflict tissue damage as it is to find one with a streamlined shape. Fortunately, there are many proven designs that can satisfy both of these important objectives.

Finally, environmental factors are usually of minor concern at moderate ranges. At long range, however, these things take on added importance and must often be accounted for or bullets can miss their mark. Trouble can occur if there are wide departures in temperature, humidity and/or elevation between practice and hunting locales. For instance, if you do most of your shooting near sea level in 60° temperatures, but plan to hunt at 10,000 feet where the thermometer only reads 10°, you may encounter problems making long shots. I addressed this same issue earlier in the book within the context of shooting at more moderate ranges, but let's take another look now that we're contemplating shooting at much longer distances.

Table 4 enumerates bullet-path data for the aforementioned environmental extremes using my .300 Winchester rifle and the 185 grain Berger VLD bullet. As you can see, until we reach shooting distances of 500 yards there's little to get excited about, as the differences in bullet paths are inconsequential. At 500 yards and beyond, however, aim would need to be corrected or we would risk wounding or completely missing our quarry. At ranges of 700 yards and greater the discrepancy in bullet paths is measured in feet, even though we're using a bullet with a very high ballistic coefficient! Obviously, less efficient bullets would demonstrate more dramatic differences in trajectories between the two conditions.

In many cases, assuming you're aware of the impacts environmental variables can have on bullet flight, it may suffice to dial the scope to a yardage just below (or just above) that yardage which would normally be used for a particular shot when faced with different shooting conditions. If you find yourself planning an impending hunt where environmental conditions are extreme relative to those where you do the bulk of your shooting, it may be wise to purchase a separate BDC dial for that location. Before you go hunting you can switch to the appropriate dial. Once you're sure it's correctly zeroed, it should work great when you need it.

To recap, when shooting at distances beyond 400 yards

adjustments must be made in technique. Specifically, the concepts of mid-range trajectory and point-blank range, which serve so well at distances below this threshold, must be exchanged for a more suitable way to compensate for the ever-increasing amounts of bullet drop that must be dealt with as shooting distances grow. The favored method of doing so is to zero the rifle at some moderate range and then use the scope's elevation turret, equipped with a custom bullet-drop-compensation dial, to dial in the appropriate yardage for shots exceeding the zero range.

Long-range marksmanship, besides requiring superior mechanical shooting and wind-doping skills, also forces one to consider factors that are of negligible importance at shorter ranges. Those who desire to shoot at longer distances need to be concerned with things such as rifle cant and the retained energy of the bullets they're using in order to shoot accurately and kill game cleanly.

This is a coastal brown bear. Heavy-boned, muscular animals require more bullet energy for clean kills than do thin-skinned, delicately built game. Of course, accurate bullet placement is always paramount.

TABLE 3—LONG-RANGE COMPARISONS

Range (yards)	Bullet Path (inches)		Energy (ft-lbs)		Drift (inches)	
	A	B	A	B	A	B
200	0	0	2,362	2,536	2.77	2.32
300	-7.69	-7.38	2,037	2,240	6.45	5.38
400	-22.22	-21.15	1,748	1,972	11.89	9.87
500	-44.71	-42.16	1,492	1,729	19.30	15.91
600	-76.53	-71.44	1,268	1,511	28.91	23.68
700	-119.34	-110.19	1,073	1,315	40.97	33.32
800	-175.12	-159.81	907	1,142	55.73	45.04
900	-246.26	-221.95	767	990	73.44	59.00
1000	-335.54	-298.54	653	859	94.30	75.40

A-180 gr. Speer spitzer, B.C.=.483 @ 2,800fps
B-185 gr. Berger VLD, B.C.=.569 @ 2,800fps

TABLE 4—COMPARATIVE BULLET PATHS (inches)

Distance (yards)	59°F/sea level	10°F/10,000 feet	Difference
200	0	0.23	0.23
250	-2.94	-2.49	0.46
300	-7.38	-6.75	0.81
350	-13.42	-12.08	1.33
400	-21.15	-19.09	2.05
450	-30.69	-27.66	3.02
500	-42.16	-37.87	4.29
550	-55.70	-49.78	5.92
600	-71.44	-63.47	7.97
650	-89.55	-79.04	10.51
700	-110.19	-96.57	13.62
800	-159.81	-137.87	21.94
850	-189.20	-161.85	27.35
900	-221.95	-188.20	33.75
950	-258.31	-217.04	41.27
1000	-298.54	-248.48	50.06

.300 Winchester, 185 gr. Berger VLD bullet, B.C.=.569, 2,800 fps

An example of a custom bullet-drop-compensation dial.   *Courtesy of Leupold*

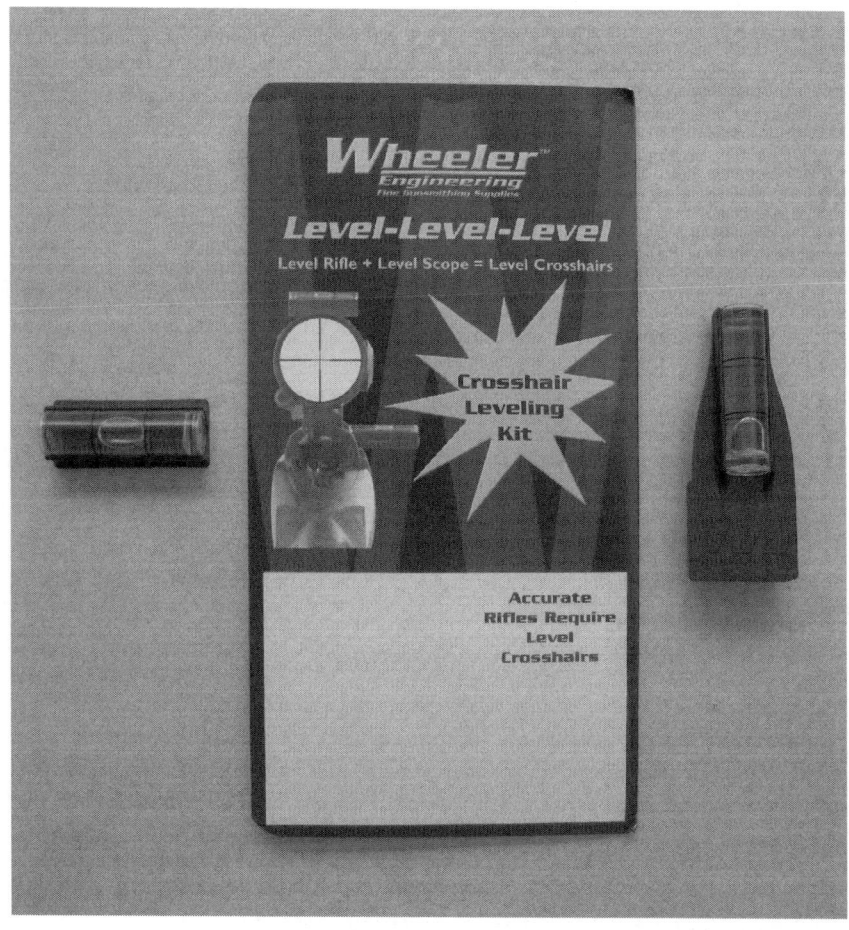

The Level-Level-Level by Wheeler Engineering, designed to eliminate cant when mounting a scope.

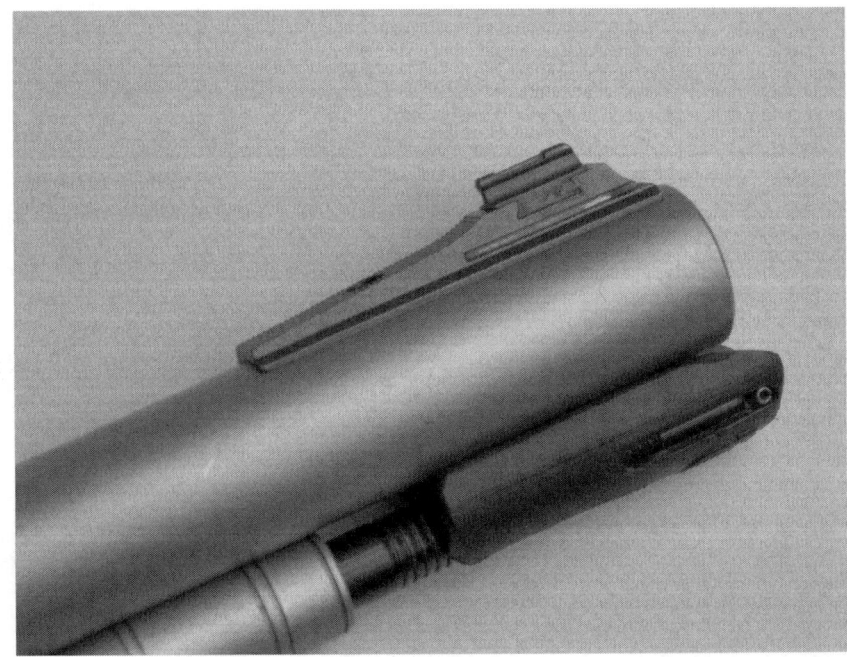

Scopes may have advantages over iron-sighting systems, but hunters can still take game at moderate ranges using older technologies and the right approach.

SHOOTING WITH IRON SIGHTS

In this era of high-quality rifle scopes and electronic "red dot" sighting devices, the ability to take game with iron sights is rapidly becoming a lost art. And while it's a fact that these modern aiming implements provide distinct advantages over their more primitive predecessors, it's also true that before the advent of the modern scope riflemen regularly killed game in the fields (and humans on the battlefields) in great numbers using only iron sights of one configuration or another.

Today, with nearly universal hunter reliance on scopes and electronic sights, some may question the need for a chapter dedicated to shooting the "old-fashioned" way. Of course, it's not my intent to force anyone to abandon what works best for them. However, there are situations where iron sights are either preferred or mandated. Dangerous game hunting in Africa and the special muzzleloading seasons in some states are two instances where iron sights might be put to use. Then, of course, there are the contrarians among us, those who yearn for a more primitive—and more challenging—way of taking game. There are some who would prefer to step back in time, rather than ride the present wave forward. Just as the tremendous technological advances in bow hunting have given many bow hunters pause and motivated some to revert to recurve or long bows, I anticipate a similar trend may ultimately come to pass with some firearm hunters, causing them to voluntarily forgo technologically superior sighting devices.

Although one's shooting capabilities with iron sights can generally be expected to be less than when using the same gun with a scope, that doesn't mean an iron-sighted gun can't be a formidable—and relatively long range—weapon. In fact, it's my intent to demonstrate how most readers can develop shooting prowess out to 200 yards without a scope and without magic.

There are several problems a hunter must contend with when using iron (or open) sights that don't exist for the same hunter using a scope. The first problem is one of eyesight. It's very difficult (if not impossible) for one's eyes—especially older eyes—to focus on the target, the front sight and the rear sight simultaneously. Even focusing serially between these three separate objects is problematic for most of us. A scope simplifies aiming by providing a single reticle, focused for the shooter's eye, which can be superimposed on the target.

By far, the best fix for the hunter using open sights is to install a "peep" style sight as the rear aiming implement. Essentially a disk with a hole in the center, the peep sight effectively eliminates one object the eye must focus on. Instead, the eye tends to simply look through the sight, while naturally centering the front sight in the opening or aperture. The size of the aperture determines, in large part, how effective the system will be in varying hunting situations. Smaller apertures make for more exact aiming, and are therefore most applicable to long-range shooting. Large apertures allow faster target acquisition, making them valuable for close shots, especially on moving game. Williams® makes receiver peep sights adjustable for windage and elevation and screw-in apertures of various specifications.

The second problem associated with open sights is that the front sight necessarily obscures much of the target. This effect can be minimized—but not eliminated—by using a relatively small sight. Personally, I recommend a red fiber-optic bead for hunting. They're visible in low light and contrast well in most hunting situations. The smallest version I'm aware of measures 3/32˝ in diameter. For our purposes, the bead will be more useful (and cover less of the target) if it has a narrow connection to the sight ramp. For reasons that will become apparent shortly, I would avoid other front sight configurations, such as blades and posts.

Finally, by necessity, someone shooting iron-sighting systems must do without the magnification normally provided by a scope. Sorry, there are no ways to compensate for this disparity. At moderate ranges, that doesn't necessarily put the shooter at a disadvantage in regards to killing game. At long range, however, most of us would perform better utilizing a scope and some magnification.

An adjustable rear peep-type sight.

This photo shows two different apertures for use in a peep sight. The one on the left has a larger opening, making it useful for for quick shots at short range; the one on the right has a smaller opening, making it ideal for precision aiming at longer distances.

RANGE WORK

Assuming you've taken your designated open-sighted gun and modified the sights to conform to my suggestions, it's time to take this firearm to the range and do some shooting. In the process, we're going to develop the necessary data to transform it into a useful shooting tool. As I go through these exercises, please keep in mind that I'm using my .50 caliber muzzleloader as the archetypical iron-sighted gun. Someone duplicating the following procedures using a .30-30 or .45-70, for example, which demonstrate muzzle velocities similar to the 1,750 feet per second (fps) of my gun, can expect comparable—but not the same—bullet drop over similar distances. Someone using a gun which generates significantly higher muzzle velocity and/or using bullets with higher ballistic coefficients should expect less bullet drop and less dramatic changes in the sight picture at each yardage, when compared to my examples. However, even allowing for this notable difference, the concepts and procedures are otherwise identical. Best of all, no matter what gun is used or what the muzzle velocity and ballistic coefficient of the bullet, the following approach will beget an individualized set of sight pictures at various yardages, designed to place the shot in the vertical center of a target animal.

The first thing we need to do is shoot the gun at 100 yards from a steady rest. In order to do that, we need a suitable target to aim at. Remember that 3/32" in diameter red fiber-optic bead I recommended? Well, at 100 yards that bead covers a circle approximately eight inches in diameter, depending upon how far it is from your eye (i.e., the barrel length). In order to be able to aim precisely, the target should contrast sharply with and be slightly larger than the bead, so an even halo of target can be seen extending beyond the bead. Plain white paper will work fine, provided it contrasts well with the background. As you look down the barrel at the target, just make sure the target extends 1-2" beyond the bead's border. If your target is smaller than the bead you're wasting your time, as you can't see what you're aiming at. Conversely, if the target is much larger than the bead, your eye will have difficulty centering the bead on target with precision.

At this stage, the goal is twofold. First, we want to see how well the gun groups. Hopefully, you're able to put five shots inside of four inches at 100 yards from a solid rest. If this isn't the case, there are two possible explanations. It may be that the gun and load just aren't capable of this kind of accuracy. Changing ammunition or adjusting powder charges or bullets (if handloading) might help. The more likely cause of larger-than-desired groups is a lack of familiarity shooting with open sights. Be patient! If you haven't done much shooting without benefit of a scope, don't expect your first group to conform. It may be necessary to shoot over several sessions in order to realize some consistency. If you're really having difficulty, and you feel the gun and load is not the cause, don't be afraid to do some shooting at reduced range, say 50 or 75 yards. Before progressing further, though, it's important that you're ultimately and consistently able to place five shots inside of four inches at 100 yards.

Once such groups can routinely be produced, the second goal is to adjust the sights so that the group's center falls at the appropriate place on the target. Naturally, the group should be centered on the target from left to right. Vertically, the group's center should fall approximately at the junction of the top and middle thirds of the target. With this set-up, at distances inside of 100 yards, the bead is smaller than the vitals of most big-game animals, and shots will strike inside the bead. Centering the bead on the vitals should result in a clean kill, with margin to spare, assuming good shot execution. At distances in excess of 100 yards, this arrangement will make compensations for bullet drop manageable, as we'll shortly see.

Once you're shooting suitably small groups at 100 yards and the groups are printing as I've described, it's time to increase the distance to target. But first, we need to compile some information that will assist us in shooting at these longer distances. Not unexpectedly, as the distance between the target and our eye increases, the front bead will cover an increasingly larger circle. We need to ascertain the diameter of the circle the bead covers in twenty-five-yard increments, out to 200 yards. For my muzzleloader, those measurements are approximately 10″ at 125 yards, 13″ at 150 yards, 15″ at 175 yards and 18″ at 200 yards. Depending upon the size of your front bead and your gun's barrel length, your measurements might be different. However, they can be easily obtained by doing the following: Place a square target of known size (you can use my measurements as a starting point) at each of these exact distances. Again, plain white paper will work nicely. Next, sight down the barrel at the target from a steady rest and note whether the front bead totally obscures, just covers, or is smaller than the target (See Figure 1). Adjust the size of the target, accordingly, until the bead just covers the target at each distance. Measure and record the size of the target at these distances, as we'll use this information later. I refer to these measurements as the "bead covers" numbers.

Our next endeavor is to shoot at ranges in excess of 100 yards. I strongly recommend that this be done in stages, as it's much easier to extend one's effective range in twenty-five-yard portions than it is to extend it by 100 yards in one jump. As before, a suitable target will assist in precise aiming. Use a target slightly larger in size than what you determined the bead to cover at each distance. For example, if your bead covers 10″ at 125 yards, use a white square measuring 11-12″ to shoot at. (Note: as you progress to ranges approximating and exceeding 175 yards, you will need a target longer than it is wide because of extreme bullet drop) When shooting this time, however, I want you to hold the top of the bead at the very top of the target.

We're looking for two things. First, we need to know where our shots are falling in relation to the top of the front bead. For instance, I've determined that the center of my five-shot group falls 7″ below the top of the bead (BTB) at 125 yards, 9″BTB at 150 yards, 14″BTB at 175 yards and 24″BTB at 200 yards. Your experience will likely be different. All that matters is that you know and record these BTB measurements at each distance. Initially, stick to shooting at 125 yards and make BTB measurements for the longer distances incrementally and only when you're competent and comfortable at this range. Second, we need to monitor what shooting at longer range does to the size of our groups. It's reasonable to

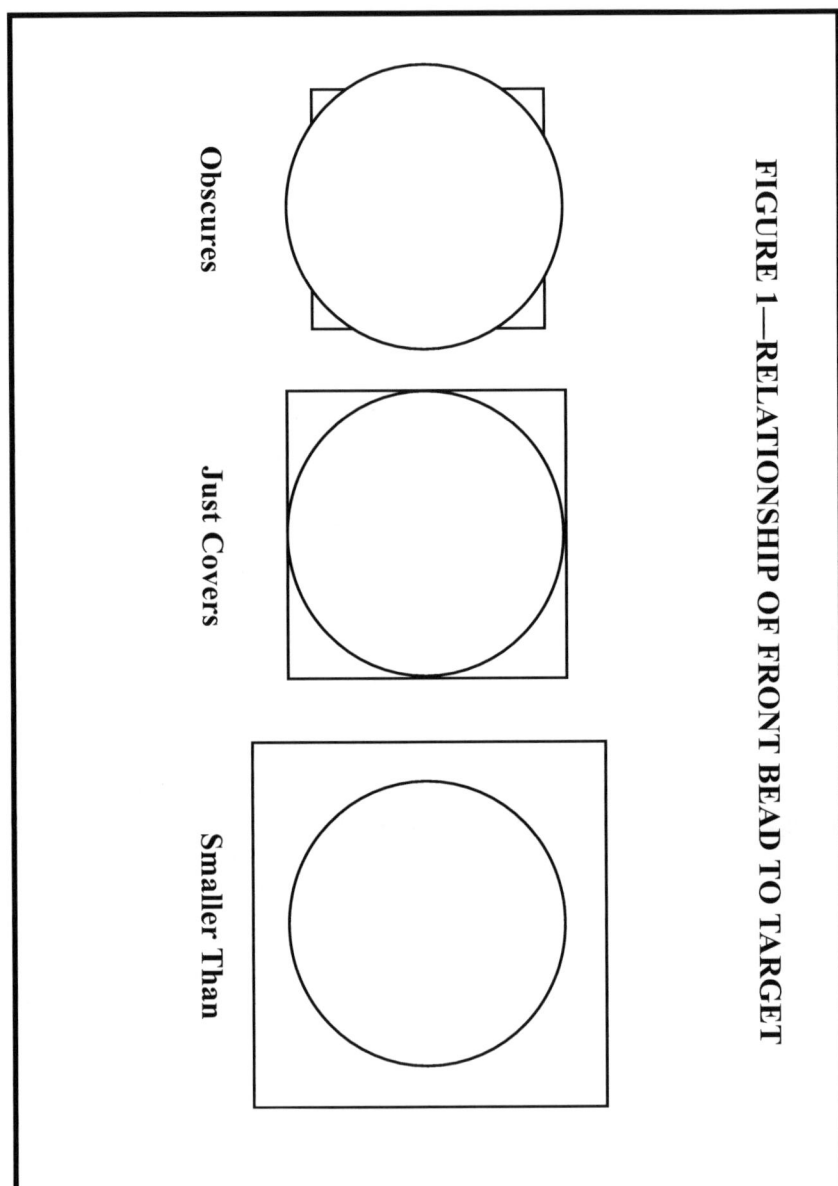

FIGURE 1—RELATIONSHIP OF FRONT BEAD TO TARGET

expect that as range increases so will group size. As I discussed in a previous chapter, personal ethics should determine ranges beyond which shots should not be taken. For me, that means I can take shots on game at ranges where I have demonstrated that I can place 80% of my shots inside an area approximating the vital zone of the animal I intend to hunt. Once your ethical standard can routinely be met at 125 yards, feel free to progress to 150 yards, and so on. At some point, all of us can expect to be unable to meet our personal ethical standard, preventing us from extending our range further. This constraint is often times temporary, as repeated practice at the edge of one's limits can sometimes result in new-found expertise.

To this point, at 125 yards, we've acquired two vital pieces of information: how big a circle our front bead covers and where our shots group in relation to the top of that bead. We ultimately want to know where to hold the bead in order to get center hits, vertically, in an animal's vital zone. The only additional information we need in order to determine that is the animal's backbone-to-brisket measurement. For example, let's assume we're hunting whitetail deer. The average deer in the area we intend to hunt are 18˝ from back to belly. For illustration purposes, if we assume the front bead covers 10˝ and the gun shoots 7˝BTB at 125 yards, doing some simple mathematics shows that placing the top of the bead 2˝ below the top of a deer's back would result in a center-body hit (See Figure 2). Of course, it would also be necessary to adjust the aim in a horizontal plane so the bullet would land in the chest, but compensating for bullet drop is fairly precise using this procedure. As a way of further illustration, let's pretend we're going to hunt elk in Montana. We assume an elk measures 30˝ from back to brisket. If we redo the math using the elk's anatomy, we find the correct sight picture has the top of the bead held about 8˝ below the elk's backline (See Figure 3).

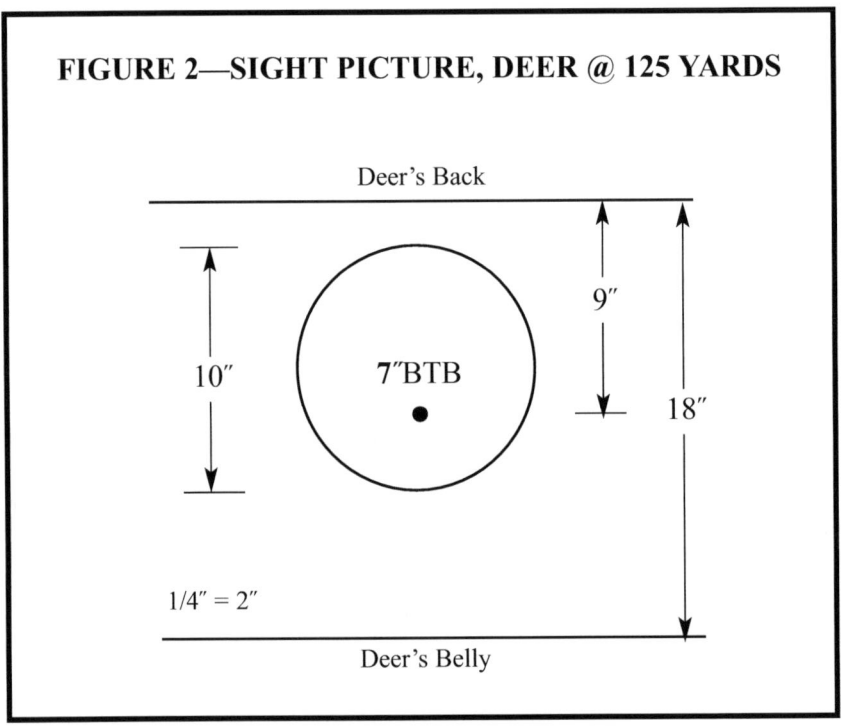

FIGURE 2—SIGHT PICTURE, DEER @ 125 YARDS

As you can see, this method uses two easily identifiable and available reference points—the top of an animal's back and the top of the rifle's front sight—to develop sight pictures. By targeting the vertical center of an animal we allow ourselves room for error, both high and low. As I've shown, the method is also somewhat animal specific, although an assumed 18″ back-to-belly dimension will work well for many North American big-game species. If in doubt, find some life-size mounts of an animal you intend to hunt and take your own measurements.

Now that we've done the theoretical calculations to determine the proper sight picture, it would be a perfect time to drag out the realistic plywood target I recommended in the chapter on effective practice and verify those holds. As you recall, I listed several reasons why shooting at animal facsimiles was preferable to shooting at geometric shapes. Now we can add another reason to the list. Besides confirming that the calculated holds result in hits to the target's vertical center, shooting at an anatomically correct target helps develop where to aim in a horizontal plane, in order to ensure hits in the chest. In evaluating how well you're shooting, just remember that the vital zone of any animal is somewhat smaller than the full, back-to-belly profile.

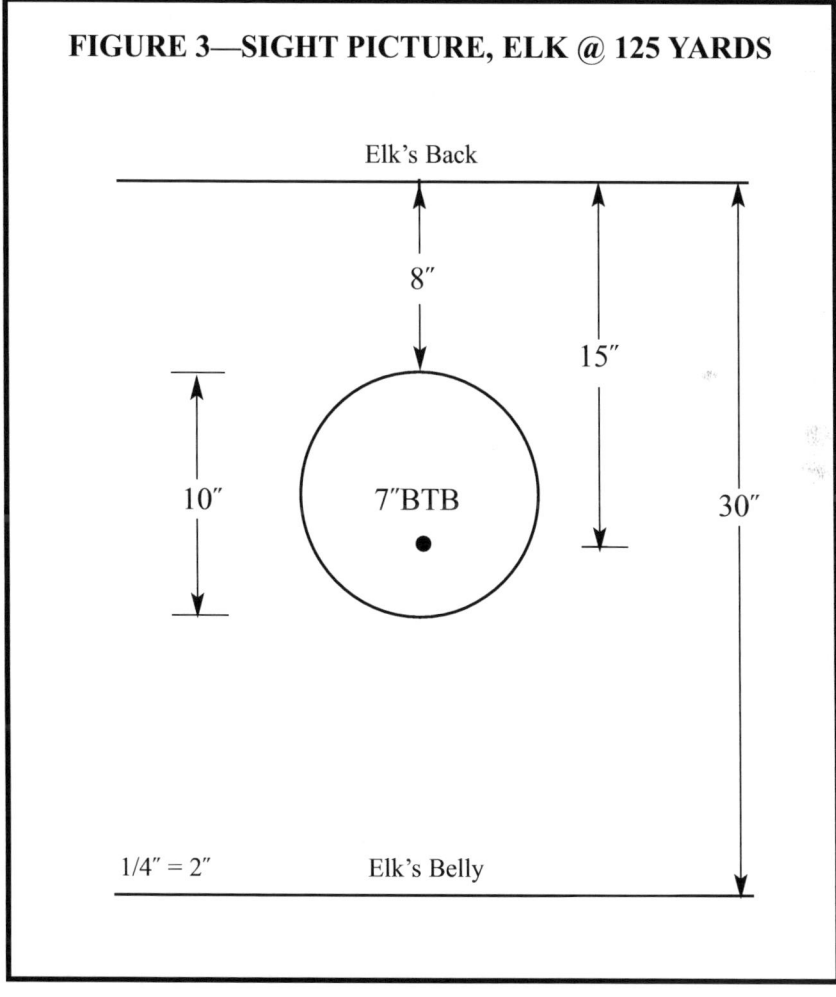

Once a comfort level and expertise is obtained at 125 yards, you can repeat the aforementioned process at 150 yards. As before, determine the diameter of the circle the bead projects at this distance, and then, by shooting at a target slightly larger than the bead diameter and holding the top of the bead at the top of the target, find how far the shots group below the top of the bead (BTB). Knowing the back-to-brisket measurement of the animal you intend to hunt, you can recalculate the proper hold at 150 yards. For example, at 150 yards the front bead of my muzzleloader covers 13″ and my shots group 9″BTB. When mule deer hunting I expect to encounter bucks that measure 20″ through the chest. Thus, I've computed the sight picture at this distance to be such that the top of the bead almost touches the top of the deer's back (See Figure 4).

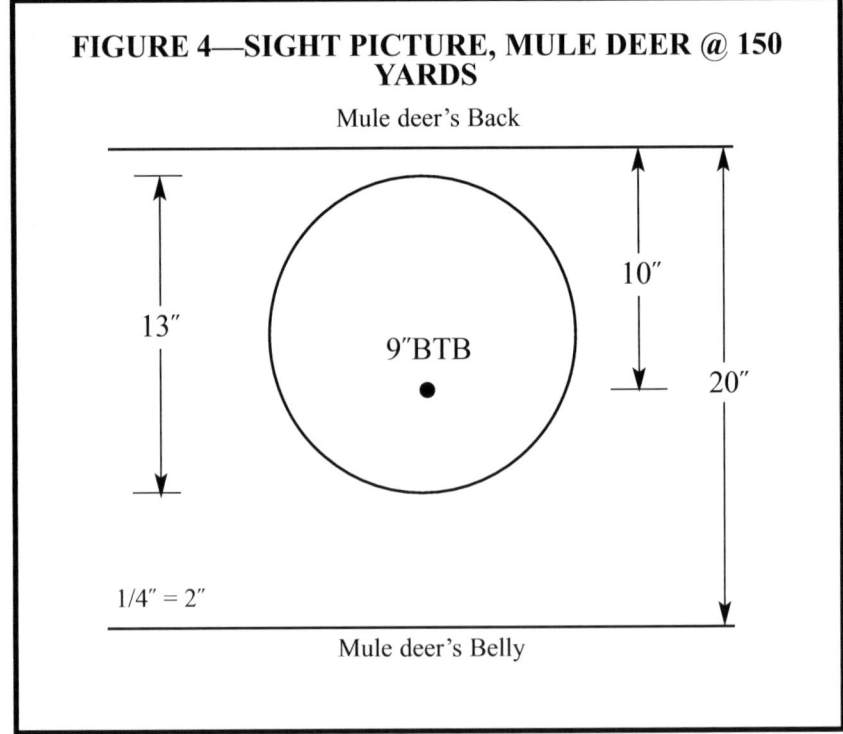

Subsequent to acquiring skill at 150 yards, the same process can be repeated at longer distances. At the risk of boring some readers, I'll provide one last example of how these front-bead holds are arrived at. I've determined that the front bead of my primitive rifle projects a circle 18″ in diameter at 200 yards. I've also found that the gun groups shots a full 24″BTB at this range. On a bighorn sheep hunt I anticipate the rams to be approximately 20″ from backline to belly. Therefore, the correct hold for this circumstance would put the bottom of the bead about 4″ below the top of a ram's back (See Figure 5). Please notice that, in this case, I described the hold in terms of the bottom of the bead instead of the top. The only reason for doing so is visual simplicity. I could have stated the hold as: the top of the bead held 14″ above the animal's back, which would be equivalent to my chosen phrasing. Either way, the bullet would end up in the same place. However, it's much easier to estimate a margin of 4″ and make the proper execution, than to do so for a margin of 14 inches.

By now, it should be clear that when using this system, four pieces of information are needed for any shot contemplated beyond 100 yards—the animal's back-to-belly dimension, the range to target, the diameter of the circle the bead projects at this range, and the distance below the top of the bead (BTB) where bullets strike at this same range. Although I presented the data I developed using my equipment for illustration purposes, expect somewhat different results as you go through the process. What's essential is that you carefully establish your own data, especially where the bullets hit in relation to the top of the bead at various yardages. This requires a great deal of shooting, but it's time well spent if you expect success in the field.

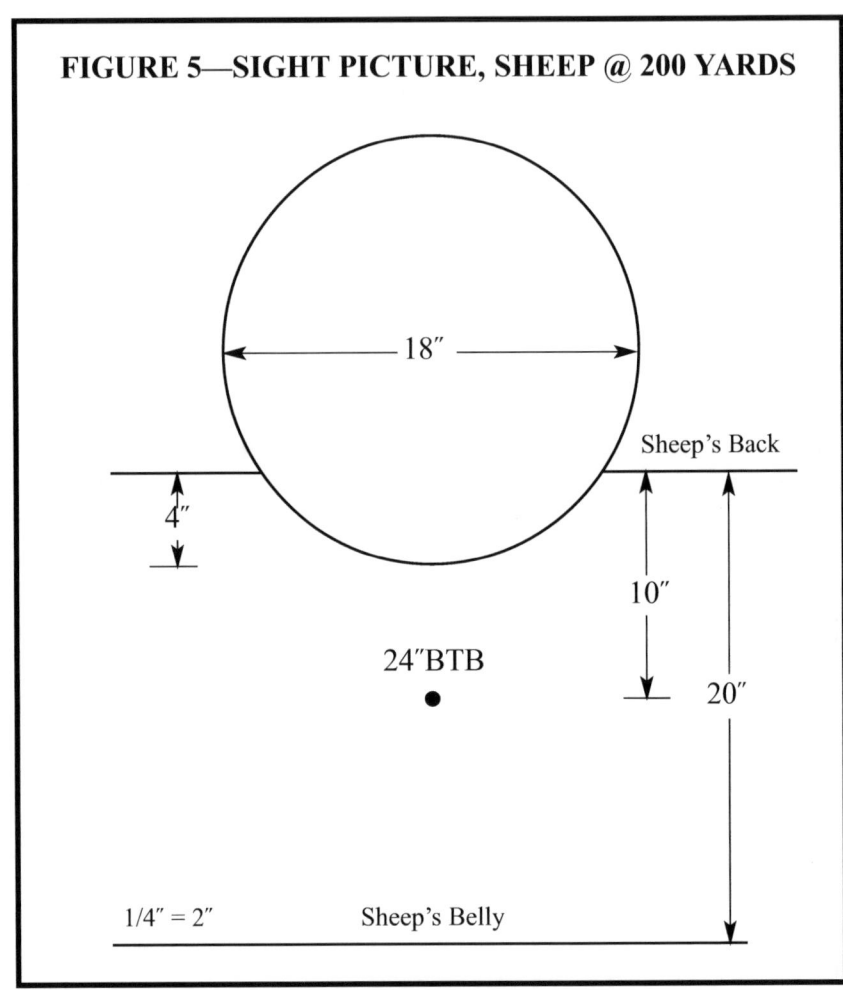

HOMEWORK

Once you have gathered all this information from your shooting sessions, make yourself a "cheat sheet" detailing the "bead covers" measurements, the BTB numbers and a small picture of the proper sight picture for each range at which you're proficient. Laminate the sheet to make it waterproof and carry it with you for reference while hunting. Besides providing accurate information and being a hedge against forgetfulness, the "cheat sheet" can be useful in interpolating the best hold for those shots that fall between the established, twenty-five-yard increments. Of course, you might need more than one sheet if you hunt animals that vary widely in size.

To this point, I've detailed how to turn an iron-sighted gun into an effective mid-range weapon. I feel it's equally important to discuss the limitations inherent to this system and some additional caveats that are applicable to shooting with open sights. First, this system is highly dependent on having the proper range to target, especially as range increases and bullet drop becomes more severe. Using a modern laser rangefinder is the best way to ensure that the correct sight picture is selected for a particular shot. However, I can't argue with those who might view the use of modern electronics in conjunction with a primitive sighting system as working across purposes. For primitive purists there are alternative means to estimate range, especially since target distances max-out around 200 yards. In fact, those "bead covers" measurements can be very helpful in determining range. For example, if I know the bead on my gun covers 18″ at 200 yards, the deer I'm hunting measure 18″ from back to brisket, and the bead just covers this portion of the deer as I'm sighting down the barrel; then I can assume the deer is 200 yards away.

Second, all the material I've presented thus far assumes that the shots are taken over level ground. Any shots taken at angles from the horizontal would require a more complex analysis in order to get the bullet to its mark. I've devoted an entire chapter to the subject of uphill/downhill shooting and I would refer the reader to that section of the book for a review of the relevant issues. But, as we all know, shots at animals frequently need to be taken at some angle from the horizontal. So, how does one take a sight picture applicable to shooting on the level and adapt it so that a target can be hit at the same distance on some defined incline?

There are several possible means of accomplishing this. One way would entail shooting, as before, in twenty-five-yard increments at various angles, noting where the shots group in relation to the top of the bead (BTB), then recalculating the holds based on the new BTB data. You can expect the BTB numbers at each yardage to be less than those derived from shooting over level ground. How much less is dependent on the steepness of the angle. The drawback to this approach is one of practicality. In order to generate data useful for hunting, shooting would have to be done over multiple angles (at least 30°, 45° and 60°) for each range at which a shot might be taken. Most people simply don't have access to a locale that can accommodate such varied shooting conditions. If you happen to live near such a place, however, this is how I'd develop my data. Besides, shooting on inclines is excellent preparation for real hunts.

A second (and perhaps the easiest) solution to the problem would involve the use of a "smart" laser rangefinder. In addition to giving the target distance, the "smart" technology has the ability to calculate angle and provide the corresponding "ballistic" range to target, which usually equates to the horizontal distance between shooter and target. Thus, a 150-yard shot at a 30° angle (up or down) is roughly equivalent to shooting 130 yards over level ground. Therefore, the usual sight picture for 125 yards, as the top of the bead relates to the animal's back, would be used. This solution would suffice for most circumstances, because shooting with open sights, at least in hunting situations, rarely involves distances greater than 200 yards. This restriction is due to practical limits of eyesight, acceptable aiming error, personal ethics, remaining bullet energy, and the like.

The third means of correcting aim during inclined-fire situations utilizes a ballistic software program. As you remember, the path of a bullet fired on an incline will be different than a shot taken parallel to the ground. The net result is that shots taken at angles (up or down) will strike higher at all ranges than those fired over level terrain. Once a level-fire baseline is produced, the program can generate bullet-path values for comparable slant ranges at specific shooting angles. The differences in bullet-path values between level fire and inclined fire can then be used to correct aim.

TABLE 1—BULLET PATHS (inches)

Range (yards)	0°	60°	Difference
100	0.00	3.04	3.04
125	-1.97	2.88	4.84
150	-4.86	2.24	7.11
175	-8.75	1.11	9.85
200	-13.67	-0.56	13.11
225	-19.69	-2.78	16.91
250	-26.87	-5.59	21.28

.50 caliber, 300 grain Dead Center bullet @1,750fps

Unfortunately, the ballistics program spits out information in inches, not BTB numbers. For our purposes, we need to convert the data produced by the software into a more helpful format, specifically a usable sight picture. If we start with level-fire conditions and a 100-yard zero, the software will give bullet-path values at each twenty-five-yard increment of range. Then, by manipulating the program, the software will calculate the bullet-path values of equivalent slant ranges for any angle. At the same time, at least for my Sierra® Infinity software, the differences in bullet-path values between the two shooting conditions at each yardage are displayed. These bullet-path differences reflect how much higher (in inches) the inclined shot will hit in relation to the level-fire baseline (See Table 1). They also represent how much higher (in inches) bullets will strike relative to the top of the front sight. Thus, if a particular shot taken on level ground would hit 14˝BTB and the difference in bullet paths was 4˝ for a comparable inclined-fire scenario, the bullet would hit only 10˝BTB when shooting at that angle. Once we know the BTB number for the inclined-fire situation, we can redraw the sight picture.

An example of how this is done is as follows: Using data for my muzzleloader, the ballistics program shows the difference in bullet paths to be 13.11˝ at 200 yards when comparing a shot over level ground to a shot taken at a 60° angle. That means the bullet will hit 13˝ higher when shooting at a 60° angle, or only 11˝BTB instead of the 24˝BTB I discovered from shooting on the flat. To determine the correct hold for a 200-yard shot at a 60° angle, all I need to do is take my normal sight picture at 200 yards (0° angle) for the animal I'll be hunting, lower it 13˝ and redraw the result (See Figure 6).

This process can be repeated for each expected shot distance (in twenty-five-yard allotments), applied across multiple angles from the horizontal, and the bullet-path differences (in inches) recorded on your cheat sheet (See Figure 7). I refer to these bullet-path differences as "aim low by" numbers. By using the BTB numbers, "bead covers" figures and the "aim low by" numbers, the level-fire sight pictures can be altered to provide a new, meaningful aiming point when an angled shot is contemplated in the field. The prospective hunter would do well to practice making these mental sight-picture manipulations before they are needed on an actual hunt. Of course, the muzzle velocity and ballistic coefficient of the bullet are needed to make ballistic comparisons, as well as the distance to target and the shooting angle. Furthermore, attention to detail is required when manipulat-

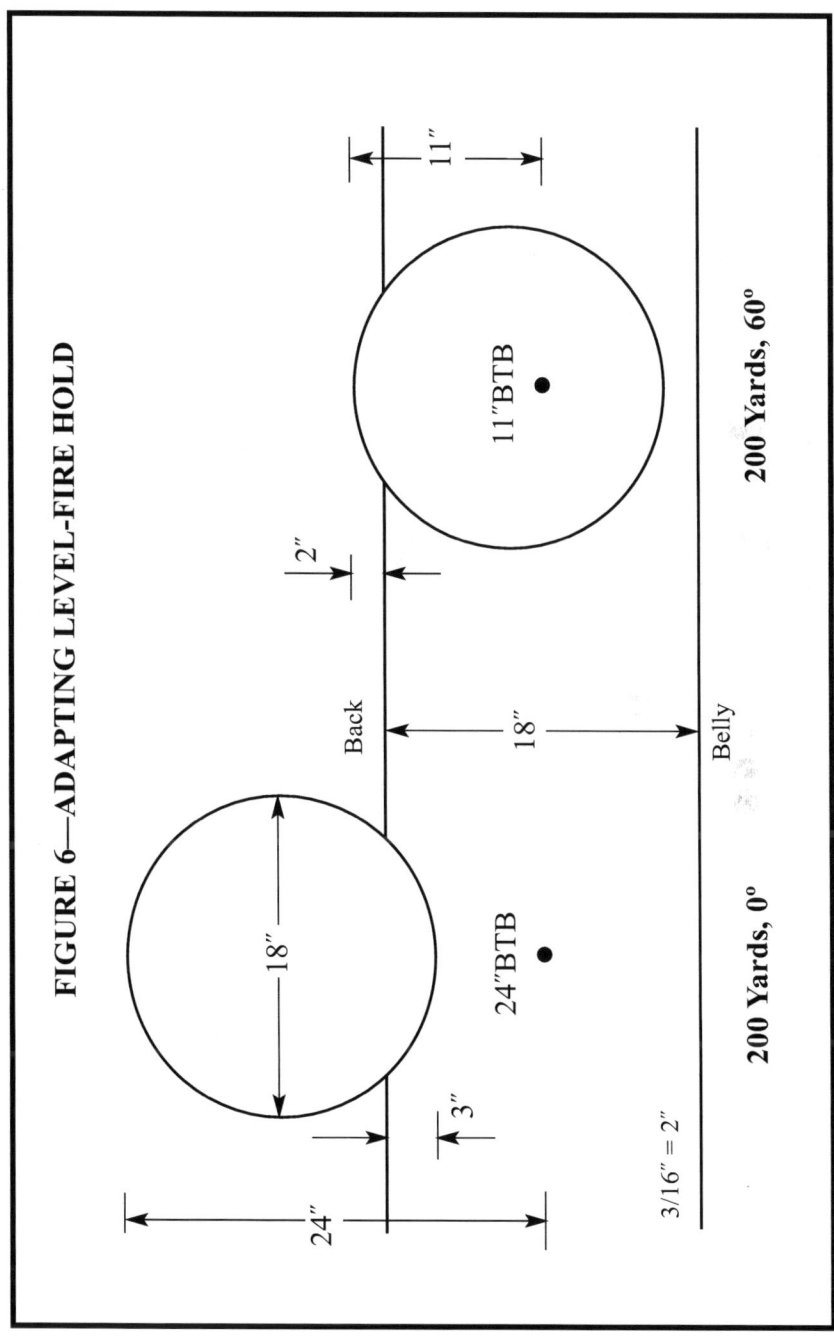

ing the program. Otherwise, it's possible to inadvertently produce erroneous or irrelevant data.

One more thing: you may have noticed that the approach used here is different than the one I employed to adjust aim in the chapter on inclined fire. As you recall, there I used the actual bullet paths to correct aim. It's equally valid to use the difference in bullet paths between the level-fire baseline and an inclined-fire situation to adjust the level-fire hold. Let me prove it. Referring back to the .300 Winchester round used for the mountain goat hunt, for a 400-yard shot over level ground, the ballistic software gives the bullet path as -17.36 inches. If we were to shoot at a 30° angle at the same slant range, the bullet path would be -11.64 inches. The difference in bullet paths is 5.72 inches. If we corrected aim directly from the inclined-fire bullet path, we would elevate aim 11.64 inches to hit where we wanted. But, it would be just as legitimate to recognize that a shot of 400 yards at a 30° angle would result in the bullet being 5.72″ higher than the expected level-fire trajectory of -17.36 inches. So instead of aiming 17.36″ high, the correct hold would involve only aiming 11.64″ high (17.36 − 5.72). In either case, the exact same (correct) aiming adjustment is arrived at. The reason for using the latter approach in this chapter is that it better suits our needs, due to the aiming convention (BTB) we've employed.

While I've chosen 200 yards as a realistic goal for shooting with open sights, it's just a number. Some will be hard pressed to be become proficient at this distance. Others, with sufficient practice, may be capable at longer ranges. No matter the end point, however, one or more factors will ultimately conspire to limit one's ability to extend their shooting range further. Insufficient remaining bullet energy to cleanly kill an animal, extreme bullet drop, the front sight covering so much real estate that aiming becomes impractical, and personal ethical concerns about reliable bullet placement top the list of potential limiters. By following the techniques in this chapter, I'm optimistic that no matter when that point comes and the potential for growth has been exhausted, each practitioner will have extended his or her capabilities for shooting with iron sights well beyond their initial starting point.

I took this desert sheep at 150 yards with my open-sighted muzzleloader. You can see where a small amount of blood has dripped from the bullet hole behind the front leg, in the vertical center of the animal.

FIGURE 7—CHEAT SHEET

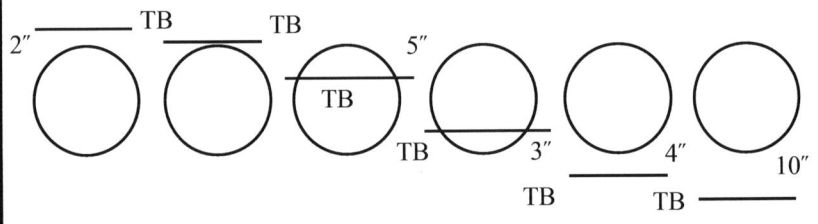

125	150	175	200	225	250
7"BTB	9"BTB	14"BTB	24"BTB	33"BTB	41"BTB
BC10"	BC13"	BC15"	BC18"	BC20"	BC23"

	30°	45°	60°	75°	
100	1"	2"	3"	5"	
125	1"	3"	5"	7"	
150	2"	4"	7"	11"	AIM
175	3"	6"	10"	15"	LOW
200	4"	8"	13"	20"	BY
225	5"	10"	17"	25"	
250	6"	12"	21"	32"	

10MPH CROSSWIND
4" @ 150
7" @ 200
11" @ 250

When you look through your peep sight at the deer feeding at the far edge of the field, this is what you see. The front bead just covers the deer's body from back to belly. Since you estimate this dimension to be 18″ for this species and you know the bead covers 18″ at 200 yards, you can conclude the deer is about 200 yards away.

Rangefinders can give accurate distances to target animals, as well as providing the shooting angle. This is Leupold's RX-IV model.

Courtesy of Leupold

FINDING THE RANGE

There are many shooting situations that require a fairly accurate estimate of the range to target if a bullet is to be precisely placed. Certainly at longer range, as the rate at which a bullet drops increases, ranging errors take on added significance. The same is true for slower projectiles, such as bullets fired from muzzleloaders, at more moderate shooting distances. For instance, if I were using my muzzleloader and I guessed the range to be 225 yards and used the appropriate sight picture for that distance, but in actuality the range was only 200 yards, my shot would hit seven inches high and might result in a complete miss. Thus, at least in this circumstance, a ranging error of just twenty-five yards becomes critical. Yet, despite its importance, range estimation is a skill very few of us have developed to any significant degree. Many of us may not even be able to routinely range an animal to within 100 yards, especially in unfamiliar surroundings and at longer target distances.

To be sure, by incorporating the concepts of point-blank range and mid-range trajectory when sighting our rifles, we needn't be concerned with range estimation until the point-blank range of our equipment has been exceeded, at least in theory. But, how is one to know when that point is reached, absent some reliable way of determining the distance to target? Let's examine the viable means of quantifying target distances in the field.

RANGEFINDERS

Previously, I've spoken about—and recommended the use of—laser rangefinders. And, I'm tempted to end this chapter right here. But, I've also mentioned the need to have some back-up method of estimating range because, no matter how great I think these devices are, they don't always work! As I've stated previously, these tools can fail to function, rain and snow can interfere with accurate readings, and the batteries that power them can run out of gas at the most inconvenient of times. Before moving on to alternate means of estimating range, however, let's spend a few moments elaborating on the modern laser rangefinder.

Simply put, a laser rangefinder emits a beam of light, measures the time it takes for this light to strike a reflective object and return, and subsequently computes the range of the object based on the data it receives and the speed of light, which is a constant. The invention of this technology dates to the 1960s, and like so many other things, it saw military and industrial use prior to being available—and affordable—for civilian applications, like hunting and shooting. To be sure, another important impediment to widespread use by the hunting public was portability. By the late 1980s, the financial and size issues had been substantially resolved, and the first models designed for hunting and shooting applications began appearing on dealer's shelves.

Since then, there has been an increase in the number of manufacturers offering products, as well as an evolution in the products, themselves. For instance, available models have generally trended towards smaller, more ergonomic designs with the capability of ranging at longer distances. Range-finding binoculars, utilizing the same technology, are also available from some makers. In addition, the newer, "smart" technologies have allowed for the incorporation of inclinometers, providing the user with the added capabilities of shooting angle determination and computed aiming corrections for inclined-fire situations. Who knows what further improvements can be expected down the road?

Let's look at how these devices can best be used to advantage, as well as their inherent limitations. First, rangefinders are rated according to the distances they can accurately range. Thus, models are often advertised as being capable of ranging to 900, 1,200 or 1,500 yards, as examples. Be mindful, these are maximum ranges, those using a highly reflective target to measure. While most rangefinders are accurate to within +/- one yard when they produce a reading, this ability requires the light beam to reflect off a target and return to the instrument. If an object to be ranged isn't very reflective, then you might not get a reading, at least at longer distances. Therefore, rangefinder performance in a hunting situation rarely duplicates that espoused by the manufacturer, because the objects that are available to range, like animals and clumps of trees, lack ideal reflectivity. Because these natural things are inherently less reflective, it's reasonable to expect a diminishment in the distances that can be effectively ranged while hunting. In general, shiny targets are more reflective than dull ones; brightly colored objects are more reflective than are dark objects; and larger targets are more easily ranged than are smaller targets.

To be fair, most manufacturers supply honest information regarding their product's ability to range non-reflective things; they just don't use this data as their main selling point. In truth, a given rangefinder may only have a ranging capability on non-reflective objects of one-half to one-third that distance promoted for reflective targets. For example, the Leupold® RX™-IV rangefinder, which I happen to own, is rated to 1,500 yards on reflective targets, but a close examination of the company's literature reveals only a 900-yard capability on things such as trees and an 800-yard limit on most animals. The bottom line is this: when contemplating a purchase, understand these limitations and buy a tool that is capable of ranging those objects that are likely to be available while hunting, at ranges well beyond those of any anticipated shots. In this arena, extra capacity is a good thing.

I mentioned earlier that rangefinders may not provide accurate readings when it's raining or snowing. That's because these conditions can interfere with the necessary light transmission to the target and back that must occur in order to calculate distance. Naturally, downpours and heavy snowfall will have more of an impact in this regard than will a few rain drops or snow flakes. Higher-quality rangefinders often have a so-called "rain" mode incorporated into their design as a means of overcoming the interference caused by precipitation. How effective these features may be in any particular situation, I can't say. I would expect the rain mode to provide better performance in wet conditions than the standard mode. Ultimately, however, the user must determine whether the information supplied by the rangefinder makes any sense. You should suspect your rangefinder's accuracy and reliability whenever it's feeding you data that seems to belie common sense.

Similar to a rain mode, some products also have a mode that ignores objects close to the device, while retaining the ability to range targets farther away. This capability can be helpful in situations where there are trees or brush near the hunter that could possibly interfere with obtaining an accurate reading on an animal at some greater distance.

The fact that rangefinders are powered by batteries should be of some concern to all who contemplate their use. As a practical matter, though, with a little advance planning, rarely should this concern rise to the level of crisis. Before going on a hunting trip, swap out the existing battery for a fresh, unused one. In addition, carry at least one pristine spare with you at all times. These steps should ensure that a minimum of two fully charged batteries are available for each hunt, which should suffice for most circumstances. Bear in mind that extreme cold can seriously degrade battery life, so you may need to insulate your rangefinder and its power supply from the cold when hunting in such conditions.

As mentioned previously, many of the newer rangefinders have the ability to determine shooting angle and provide aiming corrections for inclined-fire situations. While knowledge of the correct shooting angle is an important piece of information to have at one's disposal, caution is warranted in regards to any aiming adjustments suggested by the rangefinder. First, the rangefinder may calculate adjustments to aim by computing the equivalent horizontal distance to the target. Essentially, this approach involves the application of the Rifleman's Rule, which I discussed in the chapter on inclined fire. As you may remember, this method doesn't perfectly predict bullet paths when shooting uphill or downhill, especially at steep angles and ranges in excess of 400 yards. However, its application is certainly an improvement over using level-fire data, and it will produce reasonably accurate corrections for many situations.

Additionally, assuming it has the capability, a rangefinder computes hold data based on a few generic ballistic models. This forces the user to select the model that most closely matches their particular cartridge. As I've explained many times before, a bullet's trajectory is dependent on its ballistic coefficient and its muzzle velocity, which will likely differ from any generic ballistic model. In order to shoot as accurately as possible, it's preferable to use bullet-path data developed specifically for the ammunition that's being used, avoiding generic ballistic models. Consequently, I would be comfortable using the rangefinder to give me the shooting angle and slant range to the target, but use other means to provide an accurate firing solution. Thus, as I've also stated on other occasions, I recommend the development of a cheat sheet for use in the field. This sheet should contain relevant bullet-path data derived from a ballistic software program, which can then be accessed to help determine a suitable aiming point or the specific setting at which the scope's elevation turret should be dialed.

Finally, whether one uses a rangefinder at all is very much a personal decision. Some feel their use provides an unfair advantage, especially if one's hunting style can be described as primitive (i.e., bow or muzzleloader). Conversely, rangefinder advocates argue that their use reduces the likelihood of shots being taken at distances in excess of one's expertise, as well as the attendant prospects of wounding game. One thing is certain: It's much easier to make a shot when you're confident that shot is within your effective range and when the bullet path is known, both of which flow from having the exact target distance.

USING A SCOPE'S RETICLE TO ESTIMATE RANGE

I've previously detailed how a scope's reticle can be utilized in long-range shooting. In that instance, I discussed reticles specifically designed for that purpose. And while it's also true that special-purpose reticles with range-finding capabilities exist, I'm going to focus on how range can be estimated employing commonly used reticles. Although I will confine this study to one particular design from one manufacturer, the approach would be similar for any other comparable product.

One of the more popular reticle configurations for big-game hunting consists of cross hairs that are heavier towards the periphery of the scope, but are narrow towards the center of the scope. Leupold® is a well-respected scope manufacturer. Their trademarked reticle design which fits this description is called Duplex® (See Figure 1). You may be surprised to know that besides providing a visually appealing means of aiming, there is much potential information that can be gleaned from this particular reticle. For example, for Leupold's VX®-3 model, 4.5-14 variable-power scope set on fourteen power, the thin wires cover (or subtend) 0.2 inches at 100 yards, the heavy sections subtend 0.5 inches at 100 yards, and the entire thin opening (vertically or horizontally) subtends 5.4 inches at 100 yards. Set on 4.5 magnification, the same scope has subtension values (100 yards) of 0.5 inches for the thin sections, 1.5 inches for the heavy sections, and 16.1 inches for the thin opening.

FIGURE 1--DUPLEX RETICLE

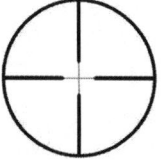

Leupold's Duplex reticle, consisting of heavy sections, thin sections and the thin opening (distance between heavy sections). *Courtesy of Leupold*

So, how do we put this information to good use? First, I'm sure everyone noticed that subtensions are dependent on a scope's magnification setting, at least for this particular scope. Second, from the data we already have in hand, we can infer two additional things which may be of use. Generally speaking, if the entire section occupied by thin wires (thin opening) equates to "X" inches at some range, then one-half of that section equals "X/2" inches at the same distance. In addition, the previously listed subtensions are at 100 yards. Double the target distance to 200 yards and the subtensions will be doubled also. If the target distance is tripled, the subtensions are tripled, and so on.

The next piece of information we need is some convenient anatomical dimension for the animal being hunted. We can use anything at our disposal, but whatever is used should be very consistent from animal to animal. That means things like antler spread, which varies widely, wouldn't be suitable. Let's stick with something I used repeatedly in the last chapter—the animal's back-to-belly measurement, which is fairly predictable. For illustration purposes, we can pretend we'll be hunting whitetail deer, and assume the bucks we're after measure 16" from back to belly. Knowing this, every time we contemplate taking a shot we have a constant reference point which can be used to estimate range.

The trick now is to develop a means of measuring sixteen inches at all shooting ranges, using the subtension data applicable to our scope. To begin, let's try and find something that works in hundred-yard increments. With the scope set on 4.5 power, the entire thin opening measures 16.1 inches at 100 yards. Therefore, if you were to look through the scope while it was set at this magnification, and the buck (back to belly) just filled the portion of the reticle between the thick cross hairs, then you could assume the buck was located 100 yards away.

At 200 yards, the entire thin-opening section will measure 32.2 inches when the scope is set at 4.5 power. However, one-half of the thin section will measure 16.1 inches. Consequently, if a buck's body fits between a heavy section and the central aiming point with the scope on 4.5 power, then the deer is 200 yards away.

To find something that works for 300 yards, let's switch gears slightly. If you remember, the thin opening fills 5.4 inches at 100 yards with the scope set on 14 power. At 300 yards and the same scope setting, the thin opening will subtend 16.2 inches (5.4 x 3). So, if the buck's chest fits between the heavy sections with the power cranked up to fourteen, the buck is 300 yards distant. Obviously, if he only filled one-half of the thin opening, he would be 600 yards away.

In order to make a determination that a deer is 400 yards away, we could use a couple of different approaches. We could go back to 4.5 power, using one-fourth of the thin opening (one-half of half the opening) as our yardstick. Doing so means we're unable to accurately bracket the deer between two easily identifiable points of the scope's reticle, which could result in more error than is desirable. Alternatively, we could use the scope's highest magnification. At 400 yards the thin opening will subtend 21.6 inches (5.4 x 4), so we would expect to see 5-6 inches of space in addition to the deer's body between the heavy sections. This approach presents problems also, as estimating half a foot of air is tough. But, what if the power ring were set to a magnification lower than fourteen? Wouldn't it be reasonable to expect that at some power we could find a means of bracketing the deer?

Although subtension values aren't available for intermediate magnification values, they can be determined with a little effort. Place a target consisting of one-inch squares exactly 100 yards away. With the gun solidly positioned, look through the scope at any power setting and make note of the number of squares the thin opening occupies. Besides being able to verify the manufacturer's subtension values for the highest and lowest powers, it should be possible to "fill in the blanks" for the remaining magnifications. In Table 1, I've detailed the subtension values of the thin opening at all powers, from 4.5 to 14, for the scope we're discussing.

Returning to our range-finding project equipped with the additional data detailed in Table 1, we realize we could never use the entire thin opening as a bracket at 400 yards, since even at fourteen power the thin opening is larger than our target animal. However, we should be able to bracket between the central aiming point and one of the heavy sections (half the thin opening). According to Table 1, at ten power the thin opening subtends 8.5 inches at 100 yards. At 400 yards the same opening covers 34 inches (8.5 x 4), and one-half the thin opening subtends seventeen inches. Therefore, if we were to set the power ring on ten and the deer slightly under-filled one-half the thin opening, it would be reasonable to conclude the animal was 400 yards distant.

In order to finish our exercise, we only need to find a way to bracket sixteen inches at 500 yards. Following the previous procedure, we can use one-half the thin opening with the scope on twelve power. In this instance, the entire thin opening subtends 32.5 inches (6.5 x 5) at 500 yards, while one-half the opening gives us a tad over the desired sixteen-inch reference point.

TABLE 1—THIN-OPENING SUBTENSIONS

Scope Magnification	Subtensions (inches)
4.5	16
5	14
6	13
7	12
8	10.5
9	9.5
10	8.5
11	7
12	6.5
13	6
14	5.4

Leupold VX-3, 4.5-14, Duplex reticle

At this juncture, we've developed a fairly reliable means of estimating range, in hundred-yard increments, out to 600 yards. Table 2 lists the results. With a little more effort, we could extend the exercise and find a way of bracketing sixteen inches at the corresponding mid-ranges of 150, 250, 350, 450 and 550 yards. I won't bore anyone by going through the process, as I think it's evident to all how this is done. I do think it's important to note that estimating range to within fifty yards is probably the best that can be expected from using a scope in this manner. This is because this method is highly dependent on the practitioner being able to make fine visual judgments, which get more difficult—and more critical—as the yardage interval gets smaller.

TABLE 2—RANGE ESTIMATION

Range (yards)	Scope Power	Bracket
100	4.5	Thin Opening
200	4.5	1/2 T.O.
300	14	Thin Opening
400	10	1/2 T.O.
500	12	1/2 T.O.
600	14	1/2 T.O.

Leupold VX-3, 4.5-14, Duplex reticle

The reader should know that some scopes have a range-estimation feature incorporated into their design, which uses the bracketing concept that I just employed. When the scope's power setting is adjusted so that the animal fits between two points (or features) of the scope's reticle, then the range can be read from the power ring. Usually, the manufacturer will use the back-to-belly dimension that we used. The problem is this: In order for the system to work, this dimension is assigned an arbitrary value, which may not be applicable to the animal being hunted. Thus, if the scope maker uses sixteen inches as their standard for bracketing purposes, the ranging system won't be well-suited to hunting elk, which happen to be much larger from backbone to belly.

On the other hand, the approach that I've demonstrated allows one to customize range estimation based upon the back-to-belly measurement of whatever animal is being hunted. That's why I took the time to detail the process. If I were hunting bighorn sheep, I could have just as well used eighteen inches to estimate range; if I were pursuing elk thirty inches would be a more appropriate marker to bracket. Of course, the ranging solutions would be different for each of these animals, when compared to the deer (16 inches) we used in this chapter. But that's okay, as more accurate estimations of range can be made when using animal-specific, non-generic models. Furthermore, by following the procedures I've demonstrated, any variable-power scope, regardless of the maker, can be transformed into a useful tool for estimating range, assuming the reticle offers some means of bracketing an animal and the relevant subtension values are known. Once a set of range-estimating solutions has been developed for a particular scope and target animal, the wisest course of action when hunting would entail carrying this data in the field, so it could be referenced as needed.

There is one decidedly low-tech approach to range estimation, namely walking the distance and counting the steps. Of course, this isn't possible in a hunting situation. But, if one routinely practices this exercise in more relaxed settings, such as during walks or playing a round of golf, improvements in ability can be expected. Look at a rock, mailbox, telephone pole or distant tree and guess how far away it is. Then, count the steps (one step equals one yard) and see how good your original estimate was. Repeated attempts at varying distances will, over time, lead to more accurate estimates of range.

A similar exercise can be incorporated into shooting sessions. Rocks (or other small objects) located at varying and unknown distances from the shooter can be used as targets. Before shooting, guess the distance to a rock, then use a rangefinder to see how well you did. Besides providing range-estimation practice, you get to diversify shooting regimens. For this type of practice, though, you'll have to seek fresh locations often, as you'll quickly become familiar with the distances of certain objects and topographical features.

However one goes about the process, it's essential that hunters be able to determine range as accurately as possible. It would be ideal if we all had a highly developed natural sense of distance. And while there are definitely ways to improve this ability, most of us would benefit by some external, more exacting means of determining distance to target. The modern laser rangefinder is the most accurate and widely used tool for this purpose. In those instances where the rangefinder is either ineffective or undesired, a variable power scope sporting a suitable reticle can give reasonable approximations of range and supplement the inherent range-finding abilities of individual hunters.

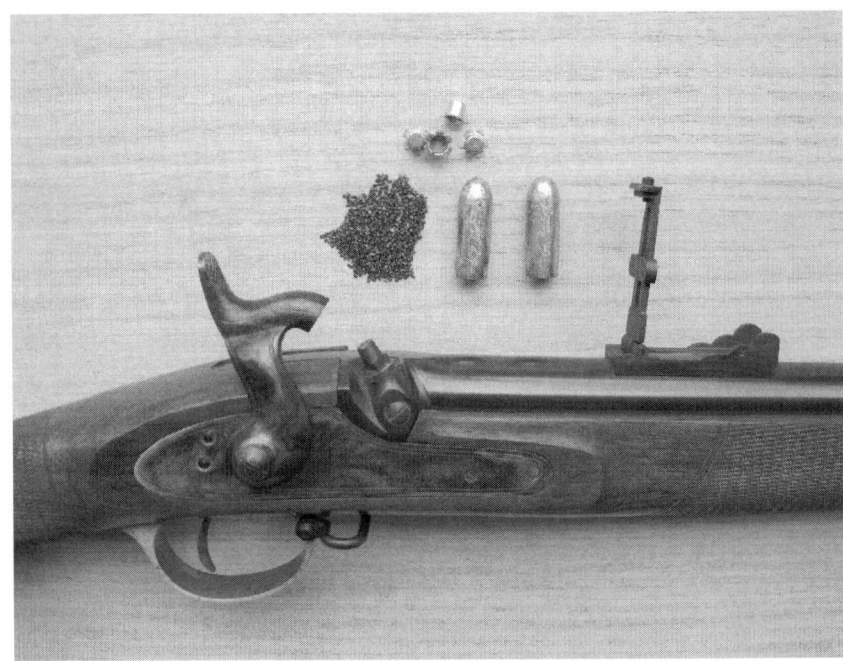

This is a Civil War era Whitworth rifle, along with some black powder, musket caps and the huge 580 grain, .45 caliber hexagonal bullets used as ammunition. Skilled sharpshooters regularly killed soldiers at ranges approaching a thousand yards, proving that shooting ability is more important than the equipment at one's disposal.

A Few Words About Equipment

I saved this chapter for last, because that's where I feel it belongs as far as its importance in becoming a good game shot. It is a serious mistake to think that one's equipment choices can make up for deficiencies in shooting technique, knowledge, or the time one devotes to becoming skilled. A sound understanding of ballistics and the impacts of inclined fire on bullet flight, good shooting form, mental preparation and emotional control, the ability to dope wind and shoot in windy conditions, being able to build stable field-shooting positions, and most importantly, reserving time to acquire and hone these abilities are all more critical than the tools one puts to use. The most expensive—and accurate—custom rifle can't possibly compensate for missing skills or time that is never invested. I'm sorry if these last statements disappoint anyone, but they're true. Having thrown cold water on the idea of "superiority through equipment," let me offer some positive—if generic—advice regarding equipment choices.

Rifles come in numerous makes and models, and are chambered for untold numbers of cartridges suitable for big-game hunting. In fact, the available offerings increase all the time. Which particular weapon is chosen is very much a personal choice. However, whatever that choice, it should be selected with an eye towards the job it is expected to accomplish. As such, it wouldn't be wise to expect a rifle chambered in .243 Winchester to be capable of taking on dangerous game, such as brown bears. For any particular game animal, there are many potential calibers that would suffice. Just make sure that those under consideration provide adequate bullet energies at expected shooting distances.

If you hunt in diverse locations and pursue dissimilar species of big game, a single gun may not fulfill all your needs. In that is the case, it may be preferable to purchase separate weapons for each task. For example, it would be reasonable to have one gun for hunting whitetails in the brush, a second for long-range mountain hunts, and yet a third for dangerous African game. Having said that, though, there certainly are chamberings that are capable of killing any big-game animal in North America.

A rifle's inherent accuracy is something that should be considered when making a selection. Of course, if you're shopping for a new gun, this quality isn't discernible until after you've left the store. Fortunately, most modern guns are capable of decent accuracy, but it's often necessary to experiment with different brands of ammunition in order to find what shoots best in a particular firearm. Those who handload their ammo have more flexibility in this regard. The reason an accurate gun-ammo combination is desirable is because any inherent imprecision here (and there's always some) will only be compounded when put to use in hunting situations. Things like positional instability, inexact wind compensation and failings attributable to the shooter will only act to expand the size of the groups a rifle is capable of producing under ideal shooting conditions. I believe a big-game rifle should be minimally capable of two-minute-of-angle (2-MOA) accuracy. In other words, when shooting from a bench rest in the absence of wind, a five-shot group should measure less than two inches (center to center) at 100 yards. By today's gun-making standards, this is not a particularly difficult standard to meet. Obviously, as shooting distances grow, so does the need for an intrinsically accurate firearm. Thus, those who expect to regularly shoot beyond 400 yards may require a rifle capable of producing 1-MOA accuracy, or better.

In addition to some decent level of precision, the other requisite for a rifle is a good trigger, or one that can be adjusted so that it meets the requirements. The ideal hunting trigger should break at around three pounds of pull; there should be little creep or movement during the pull; and once the trigger releases, there should be a minimal amount of travel. At no time should safety be compromised when performing trigger adjustments. If in doubt about such things, hire a professional to work the trigger.

Besides playing a role in helping ammunition meet accuracy minimums, bullets must provide two additional things of concern to hunters. They must possess sufficient energy to cleanly kill the target animal at all expected shooting ranges, and they must effectively transmit that energy to the animal. These requirements are not the same, as it's possible for a bullet to have the necessary energy but fail to transfer that energy to the disruption of vital organs, due to its design. For example, a bullet may reach the target with the requisite "muscle" only to disintegrate once it contacts flesh, resulting in a superficial wound. Fortunately for today's hunter, there is no shortage of well-constructed bullets designed specifically for hunting big game. This hasn't always been the case. Assuming the previous two requirements can be met, selecting bullets with high ballistic coefficients provides the shooter with ballistic advantages, such as less bullet drift and bullet drop, especially at longer shooting distances.

Since the vast majority of today's hunters are using scopes to aim their rifles, let's examine the possibilities. There are several quality scope makers, all of whom offer products suitable for almost any hunting situation. To be sure, the variable-power rifle scope is the most popular model. Besides the versatility in magnification it provides, variable power can offer range-estimation capabilities, as I detailed in the prior chapter. If you happen to be a fan of the fixed-power scope, that's fine. But, how much magnification is needed? The answer is highly dependent on the type (and location) of the hunting one does. Thus, in brushy environs where shots are less than 100 yards, little magnification is needed and two power (2X) may suffice. On the other hand, those who regularly shoot beyond 400 yards may feel that 20X is ideal. Although the choice regarding magnification may be shaped by hunting circumstances, individual preference still plays a significant role. For those hunters who prefer variable-power offerings, something in the order of 3X-9X usually works across a spectrum of hunting situations.

Besides magnification, scopes have other features that recommend their use in certain hunting situations. Large objective lenses perform better in low-light situations, like those encountered at dawn and dusk. However, larger lenses come with costs, namely greater bulk and more weight that needs to be lugged around. Tube diameters vary between one-inch and thirty-millimeter models. Generally, the latter models provide for a greater range of adjustment, making them preferable for long-range shooting applications. Finally, scope reticles of many configurations are available. Choosing one over another may be simply a matter of visual appeal, or there may be some functional reason for a choice, such as range-estimation capability. Whatever the ultimate choice of scope and features, it should be made thoughtfully, with an eye towards how it will be used. And, the purchase of a scope should not be attempted on the cheap. Buy quality, and expect to pay for it!

If you haven't yet come to the conclusion that a ballistic software program should be on your "must have" list, let me make the pitch one more time. Although you don't really need the software to shoot, you really can't shoot well without it. The precise placement of bullets is highly dependent on knowing exactly where the bullet will be at the target, in relation to the line of sight. Ballistic software can give us this information for every conceivable shooting scenario. More than that, spending time manipulating the program's variables eventually provides the user with a greater understanding of bullet flight, resulting in more confidence.

There are untold numbers of other gadgets or gizmos that might help someone become a good shot. Things such as shooting sticks of one configuration or another, as well as laser rangefinders, would obviously make my list. But, I've written in detail about these items elsewhere. Individual readers may feel they derive benefit from something I've omitted. That's fine. All that matters is that it works for you. Besides, I don't know everything; I'm just passing along information that has benefited me.

I certainly encourage everyone to hunt with the very best equipment available to them. Fortunately for us, at this moment in history there's a vast array of well-made products—rifles, bullets, scopes and other incidentals—from which to choose. Each of us must select those items which complement our hunting styles, are suitable for the species we intend to hunt and fit within our budgets. What we subsequently do with that equipment, in terms of time invested in its use, is of far greater importance to the goal of becoming an excellent and versatile shot on big-game animals.

"It depends on what the meaning of the word 'is' is,..."

Photo by Bob McNeely/White House

Glossary

aerodynamic drag—a force caused by the density of air, which acts to slow a bullet's velocity

angle cosine indicator—a tool which measures the angle of fire and displays the cosine value of the angle

angle degree indicator—a tool which measures the angle of fire and displays the angle in degrees

angle of fire—the measurement, in degrees, between the level-fire condition and some positive or negative inclined-fire situation

aperture—the portion of a peep sight through which the front sight and the target are viewed

ballistic coefficient—a value by which bullets can be compared based on their abilities to resist aerodynamic drag

ballistics—the science dealing with the motion and impact of projectiles, such as bullets

ballistics software—computer program which can calculate numerous aspects of bullet flight given sufficient inputs

bench rest—a solidly built platform used to maximize stability when shooting a firearm

biathlon—winter sport consisting of two seemingly incompatible activities, namely cross-country skiing and marksmanship

bipod—a mechanical shooting aid which usually has two legs and attaches directly to the rifle's forend

bore—the portion of a rifle barrel where the bullet travels before exiting the gun

BTB—acronym for "below the top of the bead;" a term used when shooting with open sights to describe where the gun is grouping in relation to the front sight

buck fever—the loss of emotional control while in the presence of a game animal

bullet drop—the distance, measured perpendicular to the earth's surface, between the extended bore line and any point of interest along a bullet's trajectory

bullet-drop-compensation dial—a device that attaches to a scope's elevation turret, converting the scope's internal adjustments into the equivalent ranges at which the gun will be zeroed

bullet path—a bullet's position, measured perpendicular to the line of sight, at any point of interest along a bullet's trajectory

calling the shot—the ability of a shooter to predict where a given shot will be located on the target, based upon a recollection of the sight picture when the gun discharges

cant—a clockwise or counter-clockwise rotation of the gun barrel relative to the line of sight

cheat sheet—a small piece of paper containing relevant information that can be used to assist a hunter in the field in adjusting aim

chronograph—a device that measures the velocity of an object, such as a bullet

click—the positive incremental adjustment in a scope's elevation or windage turrets, usually expressed in terms of a fraction of a minute of angle (MOA)

depression angle—inclined-fire situation whereby the gun is pointed below the horizontal

dominant eye—the stronger of a shooter's two eyes

dry firing—the process of pulling the trigger on an unloaded firearm; used to familiarize the shooter's finger with the intricacies of a particular trigger

elevation angle—inclined-fire situation whereby the gun is pointed above the horizontal

extended bore line—the projection of a line running through the center of the bore beyond the gun's muzzle

follow-through—the act of maintaining good shooting form and a steady position until after the bullet has exited the barrel

flinching—a bad shooting habit caused by the anticipation of recoil and/or muzzle blast

full-value wind—a direct crosswind, originating from a position perpendicular to the shooter's line of fire (i.e., three o'clock or nine o'clock)

gravity—the phenomenon that acts to pull objects towards the center of the earth's mass

Improved Rifleman's Rule—a mathematical means of predicting aiming adjustments for inclined-fire scenarios

inclined fire—a situation where a gun is sighted in over level ground, then later fired at some positive or negative angle

inclinometer—an instrument capable of measuring the angle between the horizontal reference and the instrument's orientation

iron sights—a system to aim a gun which employs paired front and rear sights

laser rangefinder—electronic device that calculates target distance by measuring the time it takes for a beam of light to travel to an object and return

level fire—shooting situation where shots are taken with the gun barrel held parallel to the earth's surface, or nearly so

line of sight—the line between the shooter's eye and the target, as seen through the firearm's sights

lock time—the period of time starting when the trigger is released and ending when the firing pin strikes the primer

mid-range trajectory—the point during a bullet's flight where it is at its greatest height relative to the line of sight

minute of angle—a unit of angular measurement defined as $1/60^{th}$ of one degree

muzzle—the front end of the barrel of a firearm

muzzle brake—the mechanical porting of a gun's muzzle in an effort to reduce recoil

muzzle velocity—the speed of a bullet as it exits the barrel of a gun

natural point of aim—the direction a firearm points to when the body assumes a muscle-neutral (i.e., an unstrained) shooting position

off-hand—a shooting position whereby the shooter stands with no external support

partial-value wind—any wind which blows from a direction somewhere between parallel to the shooter's direction of fire and perpendicular to the direction of fire

peep sight—a rear sight on an iron-sighting system, which uses a disk containing a circular opening to view the front sight and the target

point-blank range—those distances over which a target can be engaged without the need to alter aim to correct for a bullet's trajectory, with the expectation that bullets will strike the vital zone

projectile—any object given an initial velocity and which subsequently follows a path determined by the gravitational force acting on it and by the frictional resistance of the atmosphere

prone—a shooting position whereby the practitioner lies with his or her stomach on the ground

reticle—that part of a scope specifically used for aiming, such as the cross hairs

Rifleman's Rule—a means of approximating aiming adjustments for inclined-fire situations by calculating the horizontal distance to a target

rifle sling—a device that allows the rifle to be carried on the shoulder, as well as providing increased stability to a shooting position

secondary aiming points—those cross hair intersections in a multi-reticle scope that fall below the central aiming point, and are used for aiming at specific distances in excess of the normal sight-in distance

shooting aid—any device which can serve to stabilize a shooting position

shooting mechanics—the physical elements required to accurately shoot a firearm, such as sight alignment, sight picture, trigger control and follow-through

shooting sticks—a mechanical shooting aid which serves to steady the gun via the forend, but doesn't attach directly to the gun

Sierra's Approach—a highly accurate mathematical model used to predict aiming corrections for inclined-fire situations

sight alignment—the relationship of the front sight to the rear sight in an iron-sighted aiming system sight height—the distance between the bore's centerline and the shooter's line of sight due to the sights being mounted on top of the gun barrel

sight picture—the relationship of the target relative to the sighting system

sight wobble—the movement of the sights about the target due to positional instability

sitting—a shooting position whereby the practitioner's main support is derived from their backside

slant range—the target distance along the line of sight during inclined-fire shooting situations

"square" breathing—a relaxation technique which modulates breathing in four equal stages

subtend—to extend under; that portion of an object obscured by a feature of a scope's reticle at a particular range

trajectory—the curved path of a projectile

trigger pull—the process of disengaging the trigger so that the firing pin strikes a loaded round of ammunition

visualization—a mental exercise where someone rehearses an expected series of events leading to a particular positive outcome

vital zone—those anatomical regions of an animal that when struck by a bullet will result in a quick death, especially the heart and lungs

wind doping—the process of determining the overall effect of wind direction and speed on a particular shot

wind drift—the lateral distance a bullet will be moved off course as a result of the wind

zero—the distance where a bullet crosses the line of sight for the second time during its flight; that range at which the shooter intentionally plans to have the bullet strike the center of the target

Resources

Barnesbullets.com

Bergerbullets.com

Book of the Rifle, Jim Carmichel, Outdoor Life Books, 1985

Exteriorballistics.com

Game Loads and Practical Ballistics for the American Hunter, Bob Hagel, Alfred A. Knopf, 1978

How to Shoot, Larry Koller, Doubleday & Company, Inc., 1976

Leupold.com

Microlevel.biz

Nightforceoptics.com

Nikon.com

Nkhome.com

Nosler.com

Prbullet.com

Shootingtimes.com/optics/poptics_101107

Sierrabullets.com

Snipepod.com

Snipertools.com

Spc.noaa.gov/faq/tornado/beaufort.html

Standard Mathematical Tables, Samuel M. Selby, The Chemical Rubber Co., 1971

Thebestofthewest.net

The Starr Report, Independent Counsel Kenneth W. Starr, Prima Publishing, 1998

University Physics, Sears-Zemansky, Addison-Wesley Publishing Company, Inc., 1970

Wheelerengineering.com

Williamsgunsight.com

Zeiss.com

Author's Biography

Paul C. Carter has been an avid big-game hunter for more than forty years. Like many, the first animal he hunted was the white-tailed deer. Paul is a dedicated deer-tracking enthusiast and he has written a book on that subject. In addition to his exploits in pursuit of North America's most hunted animal, Paul has hunted and taken numerous big-game animals from Mexico to Alaska, many with a muzzleloading rifle. Besides whitetails, his other hunting passion is wild sheep, and the mountains they inhabit. He has two Grand Slams of North American wild sheep to his credit, one of which was accomplished using a muzzleloader sporting open sights—the first and only time this is believed to have been done.

Paul is married to Janet, his wife of thirty-four years. They have two grown sons and currently live in Dalton, Massachusetts, where they enjoy their country home and the wildlife that frequents the property—especially the deer.

Visit Paul on the web @ www.paulccarter.com

Other Books—*Tracking Whitetails: Answers to Your Questions*

Made in the USA